HOW POETRY SAVED MY LIFE

ARSENAL PULP PRESS · VANCOUVER

HOW POETRY SAVED MY LIFE

A HUSTLER'S MEMOIR

Amber Dawn

ARSENAL PULP PRESS
Suite 101 – 211 East Georgia St.
Vancouver, BC V6A 1Z6
Canada
arsenalpulp.com

The publisher gratefully acknowledges the support of the Canada Council for the Arts and the British Columbia Arts Council for its publishing program, and the Government of Canada (through the Canada Book Fund) and the Government of British Columbia (through the Book Publishing Tax Credit Program) for its publishing activities.

Cover and author photographs by Sarah Race
Book design by Gerilee McBride
Editing by Susan Safyan

Printed and bound in Canada

FSC MIX
Paper from responsible sources
FSC® C103214
www.fsc.org

Library and Archives Canada Cataloguing in Publication

Dawn, Amber, 1974-
    How poetry saved my life : a hustler's memoir / Amber Dawn.

Issued also in electronic format.
ISBN 978-1-55152-500-6

    1. Dawn, Amber, 1974–. 2. Authors, Canadian (English)—British Columbia—Biography. 3. Poets, Canadian (English)—British Columbia—Biography. 4. Ex-prostitutes—British Columbia—Biography. 5. Lesbians—British Columbia—Biography. 6. Prostitution. 7. Lesbians—Identity. I. Title.

PS8607.A9598Z48 2013   C813'.6   C2012-906805-5

CONTENTS

ACKNOWLEDGMENTS

Gratitude to the Musqueam, Tsiel-Waututh, and Squamish people, and acknowledgment that I live (and write) on unceded Indigenous land

A heartfelt thanks to:
The praiseworthy team at Arsenal Pulp Press—Brian Lam, Robert Ballantyne, Susan Safyan, Gerilee McBride, and Cynara Geissler

The Lambda Literary Foundation and the Writers' Trust of Canada for their generous support and recognition

The many friends and colleagues who saw me through the editing process—Zena Sharman, Ivan Coyote, Elizabeth Bachinsky, Mark Ambrose Harris, Doretta Lau, Leah Horlick, Miranda Wolfe, Anika Stafford, Lisa Jean Helps, Kate Martin, Kyle Shaughnessy, Casey Stepanuik, Maya Suess, and CJ Rowe

The cover photographer, Sarah Race

I dedicate this book to my sister Sailor Holladay and performance poet Antonette Alexandra Rae

INTRODUCTION

I had no one to help me, but the T. S. Eliot helped me. So when people say that poetry is a luxury, or an option, or for the educated middle classes, or that it shouldn't be read at school because it is irrelevant, or any of the strange stupid things that are said about poetry and its place in our lives, I suspect that the people doing the saying have had things pretty easy. A tough life needs a tough language—and that is what poetry is. That is what literature offers—a language powerful enough to say how it is. It isn't a hiding place. It is a finding place.

—*Jeanette Winterson,* Why Be Happy When You Could Be Normal?

My first novel *Sub Rosa* was published in 2010 (2011 in the USA), and to my surprise and wonder *some people read it.* They read a dark tale of magical prostitutes, ghosts and magicians, missing girls and repressed memories—readers can glean this from the back cover alone. What they also read is a speculative fictionalized take on my own story. Soon after the book's launch, I disclosed in an interview with esteemed colleague and friend Zoe Whittall that "*Sub Rosa* is the closest I'll get to writing an autobiography." Even before I opened up to Zoe, my author bio highlighted achievements like touring with the Sex Workers' Art Show and winning porn awards. I wanted readers to know me and to know that *Sub Rosa* came from a lived reality.

Like many emerging authors, I wasn't always sure how to emotionally hold my book up high. How to assuredly respond to interview questions or gracefully receive feedback from readers—I bumbled and learned as I went. The feedback I was the least prepared for suggested that I had been too forthcoming. With undoubtedly the best intentions, a handful of readers advised me against exposing myself in my author bio and/or being "too personal" in interviews—and assured me that the quality of my writing stood on its own, without having to reveal potentially controversial personal information.

While I appreciate the well-intentioned compliment, my writing does not stand on its own. My writing is comprised of the lives, deaths, struggles, and the work, accomplishments, alliances, and love of many. My writing is indebted to queers and feminists, sex workers and radical culture makers, nonconformists and trailblazers, artists and healers, missing women and justice fighters. My writing stands with those who also have been asked—in one way or another—to edit their bios.

If comfort or credibility is to be gained by omitting parts of myself, then I don't want comfort or credibility. I am not ashamed of my bio. What would be a shame is if I were to fall silent. Each time I bring my fingers to the keyboard, I join the many who also seek to explore and discover seldom-told stories, speak the tough and tender words that are too rarely articulated in day-to-day discourse, and create that place where we have permission to express emotions. My inspiration comes from celebrated authors such as Jeanette Winterson and also from powerful women whose voices have been cut short, including my friend Shelby Tom (p. 90), who died in 2003. It is with the strength received from these mentors, heroes, and friends that I offer *How Poetry Saved My Life: A Hustler's Memoir*.

An abundance of strength and inspiration is required to write and publish a book about sex work. It continues to perplex me that, in most large cities, like my own hometown of Vancouver, there are an estimated 10,000 people, mainly women, working as prostitution-based sex workers—this statistic includes only those who've been counted—and yet we rarely hear from them. Why do we so seldom hear the voices of those whose experience is so widespread?

Once, sometime in the late 1990s, when I was something of a

loudmouth, I conducted a sort of personal-political experiment. I disclosed that I was a sex worker 100 percent of the time. At dinner parties, when new acquaintances asked me what I did for a living, I plainly answered, "Prostitution." In the campus lunchroom, when other students talked about their part-time jobs, I talked openly about my job too. I even went as far as to write "sex worker" under occupation in a personnel form. I avoided the apologetic anecdotes that sex workers are often coerced to tell. I wasn't seeking acceptance or redemption. I attempted to be candid and commonplace—it's likely I sounded a little flip, as I often did in my twenties. I carried on my experiment for nearly three weeks, during which time I received very few negative or judgmental comments; rather I simply made everyone uncomfortable and speechless. While this little investigation was by no means sound research, it revealed a larger truth—that to listen to and include sex workers' voices in dialogue is a skill that we have not yet developed, just as we have not learned how to include the voices of anyone who does not conform to accepted behaviours or ideas.

What does it mean to be given the rare and privileged opportunity to have a voice? To me, it means possibility and responsibility. It means nurturing my creativity and playing with personal storytelling, while honouring the profound strength and dignity of a largely invisible population of workers and survivors. It means revelling in the groundbreaking work of voices that have come before me. Authors such as Michelle Tea, Bruce LaBruce, and Evelyn Lau, to name only a few, have experimented with narrative and turned the "confessional memoir" on its head. I imagine these authors know what Jeanette Winterson knows: "A tough life needs a tough language—and that is what poetry is."

The first time I heard poetry read out loud (aside from in a secondary school classroom, by reluctant students reciting Milton or Shakespeare) was at a Riot Grrrl gathering. "Spoken word" poetry was what I heard, and the speaker employed an arresting rhythm and form coupled with brave content about sexual assault. Her words were so powerful that I thought I might pass out before she was finished; then, after having pulled through the reading, I wanted to hear more. The first poems I wrote (again, outside of the classroom) were the result of an outreach project for at-risk girls. Like numerous successful community-based art projects, it was based on the idea that vulnerable people who make art can take ownership of their stories and ideas and, in turn, develop greater self-esteem and community ties and reduce the harmful activities in their lives. The outreach project worked for me—I made it past the age of twenty-one. "Chevron Restroom 1212 East Hastings" (p. 41) and "Sex Worker's Feet" (p. 40) are examples of those fledgling poems. I believe that only a form as dynamic and fundamentally creative as poetry could have provided a medium in which my story could unfold.

And perhaps only poets could have urged me onward. I remember reading poet Kate Braid's *Inward to the Bones* with my then-girlfriend in an SRO (single room occupancy) on Carrall and Hastings Streets in Vancouver's skid row. She and I—street hustlers, both of us—would daydream about somehow winning our way into Kate Braid's poetry class, as if it were a lottery. It turned out that no such million-to-one luck was needed; Kate Braid mentored me into the Creative Writing Department of the University of British Columbia, thus becoming one of several great poets—including Susan Musgrave, Elizabeth Bachinsky, and Rhea Tregebov—who did indeed save my life. Kate Braid signed my copy of *Inward to the Bones*, "...write on, Amber Dawn." And write (and live) on I did.

By the late 2000s, I began discovering that there were not a lot of publishing opportunities for poetry, much less poems about sex work and queer and survivor identities. I worried that I was writing in a rather rarefied genre with pretty rarefied or marginalized content that would maybe, just maybe, get published in obscure niche journals, and I thought, *Did I survive for my story to die in a publishing house slush pile?* I turned to non-fiction to bring my story and vision to wider audiences. Non-fiction prose is tricky when one is writing about friends and peers who wish to remain anonymous, settings that are clandestine, and activities that are illegal. It makes it necessary to utilize composite characters and condense time. As memoir is a new genre to me, I'm still exploring how best to present the multifarious nature of my experiences and core values on the page. It took countless "characters" and "scenes" to teach me about the healing, self-love, and community activism I hope to convey in this book.

The prose and poems I've collected here represent nearly fifteen years of collected writing. I never intended this work to amount to a *How Poetry Saved My Life: A Hustler's Memoir*—I simply continued to write until my wonderful publisher, Arsenal Pulp Press, told me it was time to send the book to the printer.

I've divided the book into three sections: Outside, Inside, and Inward. "Outside" contains the sort of material I preface with a trigger warning before I read it to audiences. This section is a testament to outdoor or survival street work and discusses drug use, suicidal feelings, and the relative isolation of queer youth. Coincidentally, it is also the section of which I feel the most proud. Crisis and creativity can be a potent combination. I am extremely grateful that the young woman I once was had the tenacity to write shit down. "Inside" marks a transition into indoor work—safer and higher paid—which afforded me time to develop my voice and craft as a writer, paid for my university education in creative writing, and allowed me to connect with vital circles of activists, artists, and poets. "Inward" highlights writing from the past couple of years; this highly reflective work has, in many ways, been a means for me to gain personal reconciliation and closure. Love is a reoccurring theme throughout "Inward"—as recently my life has been favoured by love, marriage, deepened friendships, and chosen family.

I'd like to suggest that there is a fourth section, one that invites you, the reader, to explore your own story of survival, speaking out, finding community, and treasuring your own experiences. If you so choose, you'll notice these invitations throughout the book. I found poetry, and it did indeed save my life, but there are many ways to tell your story. And if I can be anything of an example, there are many rewards to speaking your truths.

OUTSIDE

ORAL TRADITION

There are brightest apples on those trees
but until I, fabulist, have spoken
they do not know their significance
or what other legends are hung like garlands
—Irving Layton, "The Fertile Muck"

I offer you this cracked teacup, a potted plant that falls, drunken
youth who wrap their cars around lamp posts, women break
barstools, bathroom mirrors, jawbones, neighbours who go missing,
a fire consumes a city block, fire assumes human form
and murders a nation, fire returns as black rain,
and everywhere is a sight of damaged past
and everywhere is a sight of pending disaster
and everywhere serpents hang, whispering,
there are brightest apples on those trees.

And what of the black water's chop
in your own mind? That troubled panorama
that vilifies shadows of late-afternoon as they quietly
unburden the daylight, even simple bird
song threatens to tear holes in the sky.
And what then? The world unravels again?
And you unravel with it?
But this emptiness you've come to know is fertile
soil that waits for fireweed and milk thistles,
but until you, fabulist, have spoken

no flower grows. Tell them
to be brave and new,
little trailblazers, little champions of life.
Now look again at that tear
in the sky; there dangles a slender foot
or leg or twisting spine,
a hand reaches from the rift.
Call to her. The fall is only temporary.
She fell like you fell and she too will survive, but
does not know her significance

until you tell her story.
Let her fall to her first moment or fashion
herself from the fables of those who came before.
Let her create ancestors from clay and blood
let them unbury themselves: old bones and stone
carvings. Listen. Under the din of day-to-day
what bright and flawless music.
Open your eyes. What beauty is veiled in the dust?
Speak. What remembrance, what narration
or what other legends are hung like garlands.

BIKINI KILL LYRICS

for Trish Kelly

1.

Like an asshole you said yes and now you are living together

The neighbours never hear you in the plexus of concrete capillaries
the industrial vogue stronghold of condos he calls home
fringed by silos of grain, railway track, and the poultry-rendering
plant that dots your path with rancid blood
You pretend the grimy feathers in the air are aspen seeds
or new snow

His shoes in the doorway
remind you that your friends have all left
the city to return
to the small bankrupt
places they came from. Adam
took that job at the Canadian Starch Company and like his father
corn syrup corn syrup corn is his livelihood
Cindy and Rose went back to mother
their unplanned babies

Others traipsed too far into addiction
How unprepared we were for Pacific Rim heroin

His cold mug of coffee on the kitchen counter
reminds you of the lover you lost
but you are barely twenty
and haven't yet adopted the word "lover" into your vocabulary
What you once called her is the same as what she called you—

nothing

Grief is an underdeveloped language and so your body is tasked
with mourning. And can the body remember correctly?
Or is this heat
this scorching asphalt heat under your skin
a sign of something yet to come?

2.

You refuse to go home to him but where else
is there?

The armchair
rotting in the cannery parking lot is an open invitation
The more you daydream about suicide the more trash
speaks to you—
the latticework of back alleys smashed glass confetti oil drum fires
barbwire   the poorly lit corners
Damn Catholic upbringing has made you fear hell but maybe
if you situate yourself
within this strangled landscape death will just   like   sorta
   happen

Death does not offer you coffee in a Styrofoam cup smoke
break chitchat
It is not death but the workers in navy blue coveralls
that ask for your name

You favour the French-Canadian
He only touches your hair gently
And says only you
you you you
you you you

you you you you
you you you you you
you until he is finished

Treat the money like memory
Spend it! Quickly!
buy Chinese dinner combo number three
buy the leather trench coat in the Goodwill window
buy box red dye from the pharmacy
buy vitamin C when it rains
The cashier at the natural food store says HI THERE like you
are supposed to know
everything about her—
the mother-of-pearl frill on her horn-rimmed glasses
her studded belt her wallet chain

in which direction swirls the eddy of fine hairs on her nape
        counter
        clockwise
        the way her knees turn toward each other like they are
        having a conversation

3.

You tell her that you are living with a man who you hate
She tells you she sleeps on the floor at a punk rock house and all
                                                            her possessions
                                        fit into a typewriter case

                                    (Alright, love might

                            keep you alive for another minute)

4.

On her block Polish women grow purple cabbage in their lawns
rose-scented smoke rolls from the Buddhist temple, travels east
someone plays the theremin in the street
sidewalks are chalked with children's stick figures
tennis shoes skirt telephone wires

> You wonder
> where you are where
> these towering chestnuts came from these
> red painted doors
> supposedly lesbians
> live around here

Her house is the one with a crowd in the bay window
The handbill invitation reads "spoken word" whatever that means
(you tell yourself no popping pills it's not that kind of a party)
Everyone wears second-hand prom dresses and sits
on the kitchen floor

She has saved a three-legged stool for you to share
(this is the first time you've held hands with a girl in public
and you are terrified
and not so terrified)

The speaker stands up with her collection of papers
and her lopsided rhinestone crown and she begins to read aloud
what? a poem? her story? about date rape and everyone
on the kitchen floor

listens date rape continues listening date rape applauds

Why are you sitting with your back to the only exit?
This what—poem?
is dangerous. Didn't the speaker grow up shutting up

like you did? If you stay perfectly
still

                                        no one will see you

5.

Team Dresch on repeat

My girlfriend cuddles me and holds me when I cry
I tell her that I'm scared, ask if she thinks I'll die
She tells me I'm okay
I don't believe her but it makes me feel better anyway

Tattle Tale The Third Sex Tribe 8 Excuse 17 L7 Juliana Lueking
Mecca Normal Mary Lou Lord Phranc The Fakes Cub Kicking
Giant Slant 6 Pansy Division Heavens to Betsy Huggy Bear
Bratmobile

Bikini Kill on repeat

When she talks, I hear the revolution
In her hips, there's revolution
When she walks, the revolution's coming
In her kiss, I taste the revolution

After the 100th time listening to the mixed tape she gave you
you stop
bare-knuckle punching walls
wandering the industrial roadway
old rounds of inner voices quit repeating their wounded chorus

and your mind is left
with three-chord electric guitar
lyrics that won't leave you alone
anymore

She says you can do it too
teach yourself to play drums
self-publish a zine and send a copy to San Francisco
claim the words
slut
survivor
strong
write them on your stomach in black marker and dance
in your underwear at punk rock shows
get on stage get on the radio
talk back to the men that whistle at you win arguments
shout into the megaphone

cast your voice into the boom boom boom

6.

You will never remember this time exactly as it was
such possibility
all at once

clear details consumed by two decades
chronicles propelled from one speaker to the next
like a party game of pass the message
telephone
grapevine
sometimes
you wonder how it all happened

and then she'll wear that necklace you gave her
silver star

MELHOS PLACE

Melhos is a square stucco building next to a four-lane highway. All day, a steady throng of commuter traffic, diesel trucks, and the Number 209 bus tour past Melhos's unwashed façade. In summer, the air around Melhos smells of fish rotting in the neighbouring cannery dumpsters. The winter rains sound like a ceaseless drum roll against the nearby steel warehouses. And year round, girls dot the corners, their satins and lace spandex looking misplaced against the industrial backdrop.

Melhos was once named Oceanview Manor because the harbour lies beyond the shipyards and rusted barges moored along Commissioner Street. The original name—now nothing more than an eerie watermark on the faded pink awning—was likely stencilled only once in the 1960s when the building was new. By the time I moved in (in 1999), the tenants had renamed the building after the Aaron Spelling prime-time soap opera. But we are far from West Hollywood. There's no swimming pool, no blue-jean-wearing repairmen to have breezy affairs with. What Melhos has is hos. On the front stoop, girls in lingerie smoke cigarettes. Red lanterns hang in apartment windows. Some girls are shacked up with their men. Others are straight-for-pay and live with their wifeys. My best friend, Maria, has suite 311 all to herself.

Maria's got monster stereo speakers that can stand up to the traffic outside. Her bedding is from the IKEA catalogue, and her toilet flushes properly every single time. Her regulars bring her hand cream and Chinese takeout. She has a sophisticated hustle, a blend of ho innuendo and business rates: "When a trick picks you up, read them the menu like this: fifty dollars for a small fries, eighty dollars for a burger, and $120 for the full meal deal. See, technically you're not soliciting. No laws broken." I'm a bit envious of Maria.

Before her, I had only my mistakes to learn from. The first time my face was spray-painted black, I learned not to lean inside an open car window. I had my head wedged under a steering wheel just once before learning not to give blowjobs to a man in the driver's seat. I used to live in the skids—the poorest eight-block radius in Canada. I wasn't exactly trying to work those streets, but if you were a woman in the neighbourhood, you were assumed to be for sale. I'd simply step out of my door (and over the people sleeping in my doorway), and there'd be a trick shouldered up to me, whispering, "Twenty bucks, twenty bucks." These tricks made the trip to the skids for the cheapest dates possible. They preferred to be turned in their cars, as if the assumed filth of my place would give them some disease that the bareback blowjobs they requested would not. Moving to Melhos is Maria's idea. There's a vacant bachelor apartment on the third floor, already painted pink by the last girl. I barely fill it with what little furniture I have. Maria helps me set myself up like a pro. I buy the things pros should have: boxes of tissue that match my wall colour, scented candles, anti-bacterial spray. I pop Madonna's *Erotica* album in my boom box and lay a leopard print drop-sheet over my bed.

"You'll make money," Maria assures me. "You can set yourself up real nice in no time."

I warm up with nooners—lunch-hour tricks who gingerly curb their cars and say "please" when ordering blowjobs. These men are quick dates. They have forklifts and assembly lines to get back to.

Nighttime brings traffic from the West End and suburbs, and the stroll turns into a stereo-pumping, drinkin'-n-drivin', cat-calling trick parade. Cars circle and circle, as if maybe the girls might get a little prettier after one more loop around the block. I won't go night-shifting without Maria. "I got my eye on you," she tells the men who pick me up, pointing a commanding press-on nail at them. Unlike me, Maria is tall and meaty and loud. She wears biker boots when she's not working. Once I saw her throw a bar fridge a good ten feet. Tricks somehow sense her femme macho. They only insult her as they are driving away, or else Maria buries them in comebacks—mostly about eating for some reason: "Eat a shit sandwich" or "Go eat your own scrotum cheese."

I am with Maria when Paul's Dodge Ram, with tinted windows and custom headlights, stops at our corner. She has to give me a boost up to the chrome running board so I can get into his passenger seat. Canuck bobble-heads line Paul's dashboard. Photo-booth pictures of him kissing a pretty teenaged girl are stuck to his rear-view mirror.

He's three years younger than me and he lives with his parents. A hundred for the hour is "no problem" says Paul as he paces my bachelor apartment like a trapped fly looking for a window. He touches my shedding rabbit fur coat and eyes my CD collection. I wonder if he's casing the place when he opens my fridge. "No beer in here?" he asks. "No boyfriend?" Then his inspection makes sense. No men's jackets on the coat rack. A collection of "chick" music. A beer-less fridge. Through his straight-boy gaze, these are all signs that I am single.

"No boyfriend," I confirm. These two words are all he needs to stop pacing and drop his drawers. He comes at me with his arms and his erection, reaching for a hug. I twist sideways to prevent his penis from ramming my stomach. Pre-cum smears against my left side. I am prepared to butt heads about condom use. I'm prepared to tell him I won't let him ejaculate on my face—these are the things I am used to arguing over. I am not prepared when Paul kisses me.

No trick has ever kissed me. Many don't even look me in the eyes. I flinch at this intimacy, but after my initial reluctance subsides, kissing becomes surprisingly easy. Paul doesn't hack back phlegm like the factory men do. He has chewing-gum breath and glossy lips. He latches on to me with non-calloused fingers. We make out as if I am that pretty teenaged girl in the photo-booth pictures.

Afterward, he asks for my phone number. I scribble it on scrap paper. He calls me from his cell before leaving. The two of us stand awkwardly at my door listening to the tinny ring of my home phone. "Just making sure you aren't shakin' me off," he says, giving my arm a punch, as if we are buddies.

When Paul calls again, it's from a bar. "Whatcha up to?" he asks. I barely hear him through the blaring background noise. I tell him I'm already in bed. "Ah, all alone?" His puppy-dog voice is syrupy and beer-buzzed.

He arrives so drunk his young face has gone limp and liquidy. The corners of his mouth slip in and out of a grin. How does this rich boy manage not to kill himself driving around so drunk in his "truck-of-the-year," I wonder. When he hands me $200, I figure it's a blunder on his part. "There's extra," he tells me, "so you could shop for some new clothes or something." Suddenly the thrift-store slip I'm wearing feels even more threadbare. It lays on the floor in a sad huddle of frayed lace as we climb onto my bed.

"He says he wants to be my regular," I tell Maria while we're at the mall, my cash spent hastily on a pair of low-rise jeans and a handful of thong underwear. "A sugar daddy."

"No, sweetie. Sugar daddies are dejected old men with marriage or erection problems, or both," says Maria. "Young tricks are just slumming for kicks. Then they return to their SUVs and drive as fast as they can in the opposite direction."

Maria's statement makes me all too grateful when Paul calls again, same late hour, same loud background. I imagine him at some wanna-be-Irish pub, surrounded by ball-cap-wearing boys like himself. "I got something for you," he says.

He stumbles through my door with a TV too big for him to carry. He grunts me away as I try to help and pushes the row of paperback novels off my dresser to make space for it. "It was sitting in our garage," Paul huffs. "It's a couple years old. There's nothing wrong with it, really. It's just my mom thinks the built-in VCR is not with-it." He grabs the remote control from his coat pocket and turns the TV on. Blue light washes over my entire apartment. This is how Paul becomes my regular. He simply plants himself in front of the TV.

My apartment becomes a receptacle for his family's unwanteds. Nice things—rejected only because they simply have too many things already—wine glasses or terrycloth bath towels. Paul brings so much that I start re-gifting: a chenille throw goes to Maria and unopened bath salts and body lotions are disseminated throughout Melhos. Every girl in the building is heavily-perfumed with lavender and vanilla. The more gifts he brings, the longer his visits stretch out. We watch late-night talk shows and fix ourselves drinks in my new stemmed glasses.

Paul starts putting my pay in Hallmark cards, the kind with doves flying across pastel brush strokes; cards that couples give to each other. "Don't open it until I'm gone," he says, suddenly shy, as if he has written me a love poem. But the cards aren't even signed. Paul writes, "Your friend". His name absent altogether. Sometimes there's $300 inside, and I race over to Maria's to brag. "Get it while you can, girl," she says, screwing up her frosted-pink lips.

Other times, Paul slips a meagre eighty bucks in the card, and I find myself grudgingly on the stroll to earn the money I was expecting. I drift around the factory parking lots as the workers eat their bagged lunches, my eyes vigilant and desperate to catch theirs. When one does pick me up, I find myself holding my breath and staring at the wall until he's finished. I take his hard-earned money and usher him out my door.

I use up all my eye contact on Paul. My "ohhhs" and "yeses" and "thank yous" all exhausted on Paul. On each visit, Paul reminds me of the work it takes to keep a twenty-one-year-old suburban boy interested, and paying.

When he asks to stay the night, I am too tired to say no. We have downed most of a fifth of rye whisky that didn't make the cut in his father's liquor cabinet. Paul can't hold himself steady enough to put his pants back on. He collapses onto my bed, reaching an absent-minded arm out for me. "Don't go there, girl," Maria would warn me. "No kissing, no real names, no sleepovers, no playing house." I hear her voice buzz in my ear until everything blurs to darkness.

When I wake, Paul's body is splayed out, snoring. I am at the very edge of my bed. My mouth is parched from too much drinking and kissing. My stomach flips in a way that tells me that I'd better not get up too quickly. The sheets are twisted around me like a cocoon. The only part of me I can easily move is my eyes. There is no place I can look without seeing something Paul has given me. His gifts overwhelm my bachelor Melhos apartment, turning it into a comfortable getaway. Is it easier for him, I wonder, to fuck a whore with a big-screen TV and 400-thread-count sheets than to fuck a whore in an apartment sparsely furnished with chairs found in an alley. I imagine the TV set tipping off my old wobbly dresser. I hear my new clothes twitch on their hangers.

Beside me, Paul has kicked off the blankets. The fitted sheet has slid off. His too-perfect body clashes with my stripped, yellow-stained mattress. I wriggle an arm free of the tangled sheets to nudge him. "Wake up," I say. "You have to go home now."

WHAT DO DREAMS ABOUT FLYING MEAN?

This tower block has one million floors.
(Remember, you are dreaming.)
A man has trapped me in his Sahara-like throat—
gin and gin with emphysema mixed in.

Remember, you are dreaming
all of this: the smell of bleach, urine
and gin and gin with emphysema mixed in,
the hiss of the scorched fluorescent tube, that dun flicker.

All of this, the smell of bleach and urine,
frames a claustrophobic *mise-en-scène*.
The dun flicker, the hiss of the scorched fluorescent tube
like Eden's snake.

Blame the claustrophobic *mise-en-scène*,
but I am unstrung, my heart
like Eden's snake, once had wings.
What do dreams about flying mean?

I am unstrung. My heart,
sweet heart, is no place for your violin,
your dreams about flying, your well-mean-ing.
Someone has written whore on my forehead again.

Sweetheart, this is no place.
This man is no one, really,
or just another who sees whore written on my forehead.
He haggles his last beat-down offer, *sixty not a penny more.*

This man is no one, really, just a man with a payday in his pocket.
The dented elevators doors shutter.
He haggles his last beat down offer, *sixty not a penny more.*
His room number is 5 ... 4 ... 3 ... 2 ... 1

The dented elevator doors shutter open.
The trapped breath that turns airborne as he retrieves his key.
His room number is 5 ... 4 ... 3 ... 2 ...
A gin-soaked wheeze lands on my shoulder.

You've held your breath for so long you're floating, then
exhale: a space made empty for about an hour.
Someone has written whore on my forehead again.
What do dreams about flying mean?

SEX WORKER'S FEET

Again, this little room. Ash on the pillow,
the walls licked by smoke. Her feet

are the same colour as old paper or the sand at CRAB Park;
beer caps and used condoms under each step.

You could dig forever and still find broken glass.
You could dig forever and never hit anything solid.

Again, this filthy place, these flickering mirages. Hardcore. Triple X.
Lips fixed in a perfect "o" and

legs spread so far across the theatre, her toes almost touch
the exit sign. She is not the girl in the aisle

on her knees. Feet bandaged. Blisters
weeping through the gauze. White light hits her

like a stone. The audience
squints as the fantasy dissolves.

The film clicks to the end of its reel: the sound of heels
walking the same few feet of pavement all night.

CHEVRON RESTROOM 1212 EAST HASTINGS

Eve's head fits perfectly in the chipped acrylic sink
She runs the faucet until she is faceless
then paints her cheekbones back in
valentine pink, her eyebrows
an impossible arc

Cherry Sherri swings a curling iron—the girls scatter
Hairspray erupts. Bobby pins
hit the floor like hard rain.
I'm the only ginger
on Franklin, she warns me. I better not see your ratty fake
red head tonight

Who's got cigarettes? Jo asks each of us
and asks again

Pachelbel's "Canon" keeps ringing inside
Dee's imitation Prada handbag. The diamond is real,
she lets everyone know. It looks like the first star
against her old skin

Sissy smells like urine. She says a man took a piss on her
while she nodded off in an alley. *Those dog fuckers*
Stains rotting her Minnie Mouse track suit

Drugstore red lipstick
is all I need—a Lincoln Town Car
will pick me up in the gas station parking lot
Watch

BEFORE I FOUND A LESBIAN FEMINIST DOCTOR

Relapse is a part
of your illness, understand?
Schizophrenia.

You think it's clever
that you read the DSM
at the library?

The problem is the
drug use. You may have fried your
brain, permanently.

Hold her down. She'll kick.
Won't you, you troublemaker?
I'll kick you right back.

This crying routine
won't earn you any sympathy.
Lights out means lights out.

We can't know just how
this medication will work.
It's trial and error.

> Four milligrams! No
> wonder you can't stand up straight.
> I'll call your doctor.

Why not go home? You
aren't stuck here like the other
patients. Call your mom.

Your bed's been given
to someone else. Respite care
is temporary.

> Hi. I've been assigned
> to your case. In your own words,
> what is the problem?

1999

I'm not working, officer. I'm looking for a girlfriend. I haven't seen
her in a couple of days is the line
    I learned from other hustlers so I wouldn't get picked up for
    loitering.
    Additional advice: never
    carry identification, give a phony name, be polite, never
    swear. Never
    go anywhere
    with the police
    (unless you are under arrest
    and have no choice).
    Memorize six zero one six three zero zero
    Legal Aid.
    It is never
    a good sign
when an officer turns off his engine. Without headlights a cop car
becomes something even worse. *Can you describe your friend?*
When did you last see her? His open flip pad
                startles me. He hunches
                down to my eye level. I admit
                burnt-out blue eyes have a way
                of putting me at ease.
                I recognize the swollen tear
                ducts of an insomniac.
                The business card pressed
                into my hand
                reads, Beyond the Call.
It's important you tell me anything you remember.

GHETTO FEMINISM

Coco and I peek through the yellowed blinds at the recreation centre meeting room, assessing whether we want to go in or not. It looks to be an amicable mix of community advocates, social workers, a Member of the Legislative Assembly or two, and a few Downtown Eastside residents, all drinking coffee from Styrofoam cups and eating cheap pastries, so we push through the heavy glass door and find places at the round table.

As we sit, I see a woman who once strangled me because I wouldn't give her a cigarette. We made peace a few days later, or at least we pretended it didn't happen, and on the street, avoidance passes well enough for peace. This was long ago, when I worked low track. I assume she doesn't recognize me since now I am a good twenty pounds heavier, my clothes aren't from a donation box, and I don't keep my head perpetually bowed. When we make eye contact, I almost say, jokingly, "Hey, bitch, you strangle anyone lately?" to remind her who I am, but I stop myself, for it is my understanding that social workers and city councillors are uncomfortable with this sort of banter.

The meeting is to discuss changing provisions to the criminal code regarding prostitution, and how to push for the issue in the upcoming provincial election in April 2001. I quickly learn that most people present, or those doing the talking, are pro-decriminalization.

One speaker rouses the room so completely that the fluorescent lighting seems to flicker in time with her steady measured speaking rhythm. All coffee cups are down. We are hypnotized by the red manicured index finger that she brandishes in the pale air. I hold a bite of dry croissant in my left cheek, as if the sound of my chewing might interrupt.

This woman—a home-job dyed blonde in her late forties—commands the room at each and every sex workers' rights meetings I've attended. She speaks about striking down the bawdy-house provision, a law that prevents owning, managing, occupying, or being found in a bawdy house. This is the same law that forced working girls out of indoor establishments (like the infamous Penthouse Nightclub in downtown Vancouver) and into the streets. The same law that numerous studies, and plenty of old-time working girls, connect with the increase of bad dates and missing women. The speaker punctuates every few sentences with the assertion, "It's a safety issue."

I have made this argument myself, though nowhere near as articulately as the speaker, who is about twenty years my senior. For me, talking about law is comparable to taking French in high school; I memorize and regurgitate the correct words, not always comprehending what it is I'm saying. Yes, I want to see brothels decriminalized, and—an even bigger yes—I want to feel like I am a part of a big win, a historic victory. Moreover, I fantasize about becoming the kind of sex workers' rights speaker that is loud and fluent and spellbinding. I want to wave the red fingernail of authority. In becoming this type of speaker, I just might redeem myself for all the times I'd silently taken a punch.

But there is the catch. Already the laws intended to protect me have failed. Almost every woman I know is familiar with what a beating feels like, and most of us came by this knowledge when we were still girls. Our government purportedly spends millions of dollars each year to prevent girls from being abused, and yet one in three girls experience repeated abuse before age eighteen. Around the meeting table are signs of this rife truth; the telltale bow of a fractured nose, a forearm scored with slashing scars, a teardrop tattoo.

Even the broken-heart cartoons that Coco sketches across her copy of the meeting agenda. The woman who once strangled me nods off until her forehead nearly touches the table top. When I look closely, I notice that even the speaker has a toonie-sized purple bruise below her eyebrow, covered by a liberal powdering of makeup.

I doubt that laws and policies could actually promote social change. My head unconsciously begins to bob with uncertainty as discussion continues. I blurt out, "But what about…" a couple of times, trying to insert myself into the conversation when someone has a mouthful of bran muffin, only to be interrupted by the next person.

When I do get a turn, I don't have a well-rehearsed speech prepared, only a jumble of questions. "Who is going to tell the women on the street that it's time to move indoors? And tell them how to be indoor workers?" I hear how foolish I must sound and try again. "I mean, changing the laws doesn't mean working girls will be able to change their lives accordingly. Most of the girls outside have pimps or they're underage—how is this going to help them? Can opening sex workers' learning centres be an election issue instead? I mean, laws are great and all, but our resource centres keep shutting down. We need more drop-ins and stuff like that." I swear I see one of the MLAs nod at me with a measured smile. The gesture is enough to keep me talking. "And if we decriminalize, does that mean all the sections under the Criminal Code are decriminalized? The 'living off the avails of prostitution' and the 'paying for sex from someone under eighteen' provisions too? Or do we pick and choose what sections we decriminalize? Or, like, who gets to pick and choose, and decide how this stuff is enforced?" Coco leans over and scribbles the word "Girl!" across the top of my meeting agenda.

"But the one, um, section that confuses me most is 'the right to communicate or solicit in a public space,'" I continue, still shaking my head even though I now have everyone's attention. "Is that going to work both ways? Is this a stupid question? I mean, will men be allowed to approach a woman they believe to be a prostitute and offer to buy sex from her? Can it go like that?" This question is personally motivated. A fair percentage of my own street prostitution occurred because I was a young woman in a poor postal code, and the neighbourhood men frequently made offers. I once thought—why not make an easy extra fifty dollars on my way to the bus stop?—unaware of the actual work or risks involved.

"Maybe I prefer our discrete, coded lingo, like 'half-and-half' and 'all-inclusive.' That is our language." I stress the words "our language," hoping I'll gain credit if my position suggests cultural sensitivity. I receive only blank stares from around the table. "I wouldn't want some guy to ask me if I go as low as one bill to ram my ass," I offer—perhaps it's too colourful an illustration. One of the few men present clears his throat a few times.

"And what about trafficking?" Coco says, tapping her acrylic nails on the table top. I notice everyone leans forward as she speaks. Coco is considered an almost unheard-from voice: an Asian immigrant sex worker who is willing and able to articulate (in English) her experiences. "Vancouver is already one of the top cities for trafficked women in North America. Will decriminalization mean I get to stay in this country if I get busted?"

"Just because something's not criminal does not mean it's going to be fair," I add. "It doesn't mean the police or the hospital emergency room or whoever is going to be all respectful and helpful suddenly."

"Fuck the police," my old strangler friend shouts out. "They don't fucking protect us no matter if they are supposed to. If you want to do something, make the police protect us from getting raped. My daughter, she's just turned fourteen, she's already getting raped by these men who come down here just to rape our women ... "

I grow hot with the rush of anger in the room. My skin prickles from hearing the vital and even ugly things that we normally keep quiet about. There is so much to discuss, more than the one-sheet agenda can accommodate. For a moment, the energy in the room induces the feeling that some tremendous thing is about to happen, that we are on the precipice of some sort of change. After a brief pause to reflect, the meeting loops back to the same agenda: how to make decriminalization an electoral issue. By the end of the meeting, the entire group dubs itself the "Change the Code" committee.

This is not the first time I've involved myself with politics, or the first time I've had questions and doubts. Calling myself a feminist (the most suitable political appellation I've ever adopted) has posed problems in itself. I joined an anti-violence, feminist collective in 1995. As a member, I learned the power of identity—the idea that even an uneducated woman, like myself, who hadn't read Mary Wollstonecraft or bell hooks, could be an expert on feminism simply because of her identity as a woman. Phrases like "as a woman of colour" or "as a lesbian mother" qualified every opinion in the collective.

While being valued as a young, poor woman seemed miraculous to me, the miracle was hampered by my awareness of how different I was from my sister collective members. I was the "bad" sister. I wore a mini-skirt and had scraped knees in a room full of sensible pants and makeup-free faces. The collective also taught me that sex workers, from prostitutes to phone-sex operators, are "servants of the patriarchy." Part of my training included an anti-pornography workshop; six hours of learning about anti-pornography campaigns from the Women Against Pornography March on Times Square to the firebombing of Red Hot Video Stores in Vancouver. A stack of *Penthouse* and *Playboy* magazines were brought out at the end of the workshop for the collective members to judiciously analyse. Some collective members took up red and black sharpies and wrote anti-patriarchal slogans across the glossy photos of the naked porn models.

I learned immediately that the phrase "as a sex worker" is not met with the same gravity as other women's qualifiers. Debate arose when I suggested that we, as an anti-violence collective, stop vilifying sex workers and start offering them much-needed support. Some members listened, some agreed we should assist sex workers if they were trying to quit, and some acted as though I had spoiled their fortress of womanly empowerment. We took a vote: should we or should we not help sex workers out of violent situations. I remember crumpling into the purple beanbag chair in the meeting room as I watched the show of hands voting not to help. I left the collective with the bitter realization that "prostitute-ism" or "whore-phobia" were not yet words in the feminist lexicon.

However, I've witnessed a great deal of change during my short time as an out sex worker. I've seen an alarming number of women from the Downtown Eastside go missing. The north end of Commercial Drive—the very street where I worked for years— was exposed by the media as Vancouver's kiddie stroll. Dozens of massage parlours with names like The Lotus and Shangri-La have sprung up throughout the Lower Mainland. In response to this, it seems that every women's organization, health initiative, and housing program has slowly yet steadily added assistance to sex workers as part of its mandate.

Coco and I met at an HIV-prevention project that hired us to do safer sex outreach to prostitutes. Like me, Coco had lasted for a couple of rounds with feminist organizations and was no longer willing to be a living representative of the feminist sex-work debate. We both started volunteering at health-related organizations during the syphilis comeback and hepatitis surge. We bonded over this and because, unlike the retired prostitutes-turned-advocates, Coco and I were still hustling. It seemed perfect—we subsidized our volunteer or low-paid, sex-work-justice jobs with money from our regular tricks. We were activists and our bills were paid.

Our first job together was to reach out to immigrant and Asian massage parlour workers, a difficult demographic to connect with. Initially, the parlour owners wouldn't let us through the door. Coco and I would stand outside parlour doorways joking in our best spy voices, "We've got to infiltrate the building." Next we pretended to be applying for jobs; this got us as far as the softly-lit lobbies. Then we were invited in because we came with big fruit baskets and sweets from a Chinese bakery. Finally, after months of this dance, we were welcomed in to hand out free condoms for the girls, teach safe sex, and to set women up with doctors who wouldn't discriminate. Coco and I performed a theatrical routine to demonstrate how to put a condom on while giving a blowjob—it went over well in any language.

The project was funded through a one-time grant, barely enough money to cover the cost of a one-room office. Within a year we were looking for funders, and the project was scooped up by a doctoral student who forged a quick partnership with the board of directors. Coco and I were told the project could continue for several more months if we helped the doctoral student collect blood samples and other data for her thesis, which was basically a study of how HIV is spread by Asian prostitutes. Accustomed to duking it out in the name of sex workers' rights, Coco and I threw some good punches about how this stigmatized and blamed the women, how it would ruin the relationship we had with them, and how blood was a thing most Asian women, for cultural reasons, would not simply hand over. Never mind the fact that prostitutes are one of the most researched peoples in Canada, and as far as I can see, these studies aren't helping anything except the researchers' CVs. In the end, Coco and I walked out.

Having already tried feminism and health services, I suggested we give legal issues a go. This is how Coco and I joined the Change the Code committee.

At the end of that meeting, we slink away, a little dazed. "I still don't know half the shit I'm saying or how it all is really going to play out or who it will help and who will fall through the cracks or anything," I admit. This is when Coco tells me she hasn't made any money in two weeks. She is broke, not eating-at-a-soup-kitchen broke, but broke enough to be scared.

"None of my regulars are calling." Coco asks me to hit the kiddie stroll with her. "I just need a couple hundred bucks or so," she says.

I take her to my old corner beside the fish factory. I haven't been on track for nearly a year, but the street still has easy dates if you know how to hustle. We scan the beat-up trucks that circle the block to check us out before going home after their work day. "Factory workers are okay," I tell her. "But only on a Friday when they get paid."

Soon a police cruiser is circling us too. "We're just out looking for a girlfriend of ours. We haven't seen her for a couple of days," I say to the officer, and he drives off without further questions.

When a suitable client does come around, I recite the numbers and letters of his licence plate loud enough that he can hear me as Coco gets in his car. "You bring her back smiling," I tell the trick with a wink. He winks and makes friendly eye contact—a small, simple gesture that reassures me.

I sit on the stoop of the fish factory and wait for her to return as the setting sun lights up the pavement and makes the factory's windows glow. I've stood watch like this many times for other girls. I've come running when I've heard a woman scream and stuck around to hear why she was screaming. I've done hospital and police visits, without an organization's name backing me. I've shared resources, everything from bad date lists to childcare. And I am only one of many. We congregate in alleyways and on corners to strategize safety and justice—which has nothing to do with government or institutional assistance.

I realize that this is the place where I have discovered a kind of ghetto feminism, a street social justice. This is the place where I understand the impact my actions have. Where I trust myself; where I do not question my voice or the voices of the other women here. This corner, where I wait for Coco, is the one space where I have learned and shared the most influential tools of my life—listen, witness, pass information forward, be at the ready, and survive. Survival may be the most radical thing I ever do.

HOW POETRY SAVED MY LIFE

There wasn't a voice
from above
no tunnel of light
I didn't awaken in a hospital room to doctors cheering,
you're a lucky young lady
you almost didn't make it

There was a missing women poster
wrapped around a telephone pole
on the corner of Pandora and Victoria

When I say poetry saved my life I should also mention
other forces—
by 1999 all the cars cruising the kiddie stroll had power-
lock doors, crystal meth turned the girls
on each other, and I hated fighting women,
Sheila Catherine Egan,
four years younger than I am,
disappeared the previous July
and has still not been found.
I am white, and while my genes are likely predisposed
to addiction, I can use
and quit and use and quit anything.
These privileges allowed me to admit
that it was a terrifying time to be working outside, and I no longer

wanted to die
four thousand miles
away from the small river-bed town
where I was born.

And, yes, poetry must be thanked too.
The written word can be a faithful witness
if you're willing to show yourself.
Moreover, poetry reunited me with the girl
who didn't mind the endless backwoods tree line
and was thrilled by the sound of coyotes screaming at night.
Someday I'll write about her.

INSIDE

BUT I'M IN COLLEGE

The sun hasn't set yet, and already the sidewalk outside the massage parlour is overrun by the Mesa Luna crowd. It is June of 2000—the millennium bug has long since become a joke—and everyone just wants to salsa dance.

The trouble with the salsa craze is that I recently started a job at a parlour directly below Mesa Luna—Vancouver's "it" Latin dance club. To get to our frosted-glass parlour door on a Saturday night means cutting through an antsy queue of salsa dancers, all dressed in spandex-blend fabrics, gold rings, and polished leather shoes, all hair-sprayed and perfumed, and already a little drunk from their dinner martinis. Even the most unreserved tricks won't cut through the line-up. Until every last salsa fiend is admitted past Mesa Luna's velvet rope, we will be a tableau of sad tramps sprawled out on the staff room sofas.

I catch my right foot tapping to a muffled beat leaking through the ceiling. Embarrassed, I pull the leopard print polar fleece blanket over me before the other girls notice. The staff here thinks salsa music is an assault on our livelihood. I don't want to be caught keeping the enemy's tempo, even involuntarily.

Caress and Tia-Lee are tangled together on the faux suede sectional. Tia-Lee is tucked under Caress's powerhouse of an arm. On the whiteboard staff schedule tacked to the wall, Caress and Tia-Lee's names both appear on every five p.m. to midnight shift, Wednesday through Sunday—one never works without the other. On the clothes tree, one large and one extra-small black satin housecoat hang together. One size-ten and one size-six pair of Lucite stilettos are perched side-by-side on the shoe rack. Caress and Tia-Lee call one another "wifey," and I suspect that means they are queer like me. They clearly run the place, and I am the lowly new girl, so I refrain from giving any kind of queer nod or outing myself. This is my first indoor job, and while it is safer than the street, I can already tell that there are many unspoken rules among the staff, and consequences for breaking these rules.

Besides increased safety, the biggest advantage I've noticed about working indoors is cable television. The three of us watch a man eat a plate of live beetle larvae. *Survivor: Borneo* speaks to us in a way that 1990s sitcoms never could. Working girls understand competing with each other while being forced to share the same confined space. We will perform stunts for large sums of money.

"Bugs! Fucking bugs! Can you believe that? A million dollars isn't worth it," Tia-Lee shrieks.

Caress is on the phone at each and every commercial break. "Always on the phone," Tia-Lee turns to me and says. This is the first time she's spoken to me since my laid-back parlour job interview, when she warned me not to drink her diet Dr Pepper just after informing me that I was hired.

"You'd think she's some kinda ho hotline. 'Hey girl, I'm at the shop,'" she mimics Caress, holding her shoe up to her ear like a phone receiver. "'Where are you? Oh, you're at the dirty dirty. How's it there? Yeah, it's dead here too. My girls down on Richards say it's a bust there too.'"

Caress waves her arms to shush Tia-Lee and accidentally pushes her off the sofa. Tia-Lee lands on the ashtray, knocking half-smoked cigarettes across the floor. "Bitch," says Tia-Lee. "I ain't cleaning that up."

"That's what you get for smoking in here," Caress says, putting her hand over the phone receiver.

"We're not supposed to use the business phone for personal calls, either."

"I am talking business on the business phone," hisses Caress.

Tia-Lee folds her arms in front of her chest and glares at Caress for a moment before stomping across the room for the dust buster. She sticks her ass in Caress's face as she sucks up the mess of ashes, then points the dust buster at Caress's head like a gun. One of Caress's braids gets sucked up. Her eyes widen. "I gotta go," she shouts into the phone and hangs up. "Why are you pointing that thing upside my head?" She holds her mangled braid in her hand.

"It's not even your real hair," says Tia-Lee.

"Don't get into it with me."

"I got nothing else to do." Tia-Lee lets the dust buster drop to the floor as she flops on the sofa. "What happened to our margaritas? Make Selina hurry up with our drinks."

"Selina's been up there forever." Caress reaches for the phone again. "She better not be hustling."

"Can't say I blame her," I huff. There are always more men in the Mesa Luna line-up than women. "That club must be full of tricks."

"We work inside for a reason," snaps Caress. "This here is a job. Le-git-i-mate. Not trashy low track. Got it?"

This is only one of several instances where Caress has sharply shared her dislike for street work, and for me. I regret telling her that I had worked outside. When I mentioned Franklin Street, I had thought maybe she'd heard in the local news about the girls who'd gone missing and feel sorry for me. That maybe she'd wrap that powerhouse of an arm around my shoulders and start mothering me like she mothers Tia-Lee. Instead, she watches me with a close and distrustful eye. In an attempt to salvage my status, I mentioned how I go to college. I even made a bit of a show reading my *Writing Poetry, Second Edition* textbook in the staff room. This only set me further apart from Caress. I don't know what's worse in her books, a street hooker or a college girl. Being both, she was quick to let me know, is "fucking weird." Caress doesn't think I'll last in the parlour, but her judgments only make me want to prove her wrong. I'll buy myself the same pastel-coloured lingerie she wears, the same Mary-Jane stilettos. I'll get acrylic nails. I'll dye my hair blonde. I'll go by the name of Donna and smile all the time. I'm going to make the same money Caress does, maybe more. Caress can move aside as I sprawl out on the sectional sofa and watch cable television. I'll stock the bar fridge with my own Dr Pepper. I'll read poetry textbooks in the staff room. Just to get on her nerves, I'll move my lips when I read and sigh out loud as I marvel at language and form and voice. I'll call my girlfriend on the business phone and flirt, loudly. I'll show Caress "fucking weird." Or maybe I won't ... but at the very least, I refuse to be run out of a lousy massage parlour.

Caress's cell phone rings. "Selina," she booms into her pink Motorola flip phone. She speaks to Selina more sharply than she does to me. I don't know Selina from a sack of cats, but somehow I feel sorry for her. My skin grows hot listening to the rising volume of Caress's voice. I look around for the TV remote. It is wedged under Tia-Lee's thigh. I distract myself for a moment flipping through the pages of a dog-eared fashion magazine on the coffee table. There's half a pot of coffee left. I wonder how old it is. I have a sudden craving for popcorn, but I don't want the beeping microwave to escalate Caress's foul mood.

I reach inside my purse and hold my wallet. I've made only $140 tonight; still, that's more than Tia-Lee or Caress, who haven't had clients yet. And it's far more than what I used to make from a basic hand job. I fish out my compact and examine my skin in the tiny mirror. Do I look healthier? I check my tongue to see if it's coated. It's always coated. In the low lights of the parlour, no one notices a coated tongue. But on campus, do I look as healthy as the other students? I'm trying hard to look like them, and most of the time I believe I belong until Introduction to Non-Fiction class and it's time for one of my stories to be workshopped and the room grows very quiet. There is always one smartypants who has to comment on my habitual dyslexic typos. The other students tell me that I am "brave." They keep their eyes on the page when they speak to me. I suppose this is better than the way Caress glares.

"Stop that, sketchy," Tia-Lee nudges the compact mirror in my hand. "Stop poking at your face and get ready. Selina is bringing down a bunch of out-of-towners."

"What about Caress?"

"She knows. She's taking the price sign out of the lobby. Selena told these guys we charge $350 an hour. They're American."

I powder the shine from my nose and forehead and toss my fingers through my hair. My shoes are stripper pumps from Value Village. I used a black sharpie marker to cover the scuffmarks. *You do not do, you do not do / Any more, black shoe*; I felt so fucking clever reciting Sylvia Plath as I made my second-hand heels look like new.

The bell in the lobby rings. Men's voices come crashing through the front door, breaking hours of stale silence. Before I peek out to see our visitors, Selina and Caress march stiffly into the staff room. Selina wobbles a bit in her heels, smelling like beer.

"There's five of them," Caress says, her hands flying up in frustration. "We can't be leaving one sitting around unattended."

"Look. New girl," says Selina, waving a careless finger at me, "takes one into the Safari room. Tia-Lee takes one into the den. You take one into the bordello. And I already planned to take two into the Roman room."

"You're taking two," Caress scoffs.

"What do you care how I sell my pussy? I'm going home with at least seven bills tonight. You should thank me for bringing some cash through the door."

"Whatever, nasty," Caress says, then leads all four girls into the lobby in a procession of clacking heels. "Gentlemen," she beams at the men, who are in their late forties or maybe early fifties. "It's late, so I'm just going to lock the front door. Now we can spend the rest of the night together, undisturbed. Why don't you each choose a lady and settle the money in private with her? We suggest $350 for the hour. American or Canadian. I'm sure you will find it quite worth your while."

I lean up against the wall and play my game with my eyes, lowering them as if I am shy, then letting them travel across the men's groins and then to their faces. One of them steps forward and says, "I'd like to see you."

"Sure." I touch his wrist. "I'd like that too."

When I take off his blazer, I rub the soft khaki fabric between my pointer finger and thumb, then drape it over the leopard-print chaise longue. I eye his G-shaped brass belt buckle a moment before I realize that the "G" stands for Gucci.

"Donna," he says, calling me by my newly appointed work name as he takes out a money clip. "I have no idea what $350 gets me, but how about I just offer you this and we have a really good time together?"

He flashes a wad of Canadian hundred-dollar bills, five of which he hands to me. A strange panic surges through me, as if I might start to weep as I take his money. Surely he notices this tremor of desperation. This is more than a month's rent. Almost two college courses' tuition and books. "Good exchange rate?" I ask, recovering.

"Yes," he grins. "It makes it worthwhile to come and play in Canada."

"Yes," I grin back. "Your dollar is so strong." I elongate the easy, predictable "o" in strong and he unclips his belt buckle.

A couple of hours later, Tia-Lee and I hoist Selina up from the shower floor. Vomit beads her damp hair. The pair of tricks she took to the Roman room ordered four more pitchers of margaritas and spent their session hooting and shouting incomprehensibly.

"Selina never finishes a shift sober."

"What do we do? Put her in a cab?" I ask. Selina's head rolls forward on her slender, slack neck. She whimpers, gags, and spits onto the white tile floor. Her saliva stinks of puke. I pull some of my hair across my nose and breath in the scent of shampoo.

"You can't put a drunk bitch in a cab," Tia-Lee scolds, then leans closer and, in a hushed tone, tells me, "A cabbie raped her a couple weeks ago. That's what she said, anyway."

Blame. Blame is the most discernible emotion vacillating around the tiny white-tiled room. There is the clear hint of blame in Tia-Lee's words. And as I rub Selina's back, I too am holding her responsible for spoiling my false sense of security. Less than three weeks ago, I arrived at the massage parlour exasperated from fear of violence. I wanted to leave rape on the street. Couldn't this space be only about cable television and Gucci belts for a bit longer? Acute recognition like this can be defeating for a survivor. *One pain situates itself so close to another pain*, I think. *That's a line of a poem. I should write that down.* Maybe this is the precise moment when poetry becomes my primary way to cope. Something lifts inside my body—that buoyancy that comes when I observe my life as art. Shame follows close behind. Not shame of being a working girl and a woman and a rape survivor, but shame over emotionally distancing myself from Tia-Lee and Selina. I must force myself to keep a steady hand on Selina's back, to stay by her side.

"Ain't this just what you want, Selina?" Caress appears in the bathroom doorway. "You're the centre of attention again." Tia-Lee drops Selina's hand and stands up.

"You deal with her, new girl. Donna," says Caress, "we've babysat her too many times. Somebody else needs to take care of her. Lock her in here if you have to."

"Don't you fucking lock me in here again," Selina wails.

Caress won't look at her; she squeezes her eyes shut for a moment. "I'm so fucking tired of all this racket," she says. "You're promoted to key holder, Donna. You wanna work here, right? This here is the job. Key holder cleans up and locks up. Can you do this?"

"Sure. You and Tia go home." I don't know if I've somewhat gained her trust or officially become her lackey, but at least she smiles weakly at me as she presses the keys into my hand.

I count the house's cut of the money made tonight, seal the cash in an envelope, and deposit it into the slot in the metal safe under the front desk. Does the owner really know what actions are attached to the money he picks up each morning? I sign my name—Donna—in the nightly log-book. Windex the mirrors. Vacuum. Dust the plastic leaves of the fake palms in the lobby. Selina emerges from the bathroom as I am folding laundry. She stumbles down the hallway. A moment later Justin Timberlake blasts through the stereo. She sings "Bye, Bye, Bye" into the intercom system in the lobby. I can't help but laugh at her drunken harmony.

"Good timing," I chirp, following her off-key song. "I just finished cleaning. Let's get out of here." Selina has dumped her purse out on the front desk, American bills spread out like in a Hollywood movie. She sets up a line of cocaine on her 'N Sync CD case. "Caress would have locked me in all night, you know that?" She snorts through a tightly rolled American bill, and her face flushes.

"Do you know how shitty it is to wake up in this place?"

She passes the CD case and the rolled bill to me. "You party?"

I want to say to her, *But I got off the street. I'm in college. I'm studying Sylvia mother-fucking Plath. I have a le-git-i-mate job. I'm going to write my story.* Cocaine is a great equalizer; it does not distinguish between a street hooker, a college girl, or anyone else for that matter. The rush and burn are the same. I justify a single line—to put this night behind me. A second line—to get me up and out of here. A third. One pain situates itself so close to another pain.

GLOSSY

The reek of pot smoke and fried delivery food, stinking cheap
scented candles. *Oh!* K-Y Jelly and latex bouquet.
The hairspray and weave sheen in your nostrils, the cock stench
the cunt smell—
eventually all this
disappears
and you think you are breathing fresh air.

The girl who only wears neon-
coloured swimsuits dumps
Cover Girl foundation over her stretch marks (childbearing) lace-
ribbon-like scars (boob job), and knife wound (on-again-off again
boyfriend) and discusses matters of the heart, you know
that she is wise beyond any doubt wise and yes
she is definitely *yes* giving you sound advice.

That same girl you will help bear the weight
of a blacked out
man; together
bring his sloppy body out of the door and into the parking lot
rifle through his pockets before laying him on the hood of his own
car.

Wear her clothes
if she feels like being nice to you,
dresses that are nothing more than a tiny tube of shiny fabric

dresses so small your ass is half out, nipples go pop.
She teaches you how to levitate
six inches from the floor
metatarsalgia
shin splints
　　shin splints
　　　hammer toe
　　　　shin splints
　　　　tendonitis
　　　　　neuromas
　　　　　　shin splints
　　　　　　Achilles
　　　　　　　ingrown
　　　　　　　bunion
　　　　　　　　callous
　　　　　　　　corns

study the Adam's apple
the visceral movement of the many
men who say nothing to you
or they clear their throats
they are not accustomed to this climate
or to standing naked while their eyes adjust in black light
　　　you favour the nervous
　　　somehow their goose bumps remind you
　　　of kissing the back of your hand
to these men you'll give more than what they ask for

WHAT'S MY MOTHER F***ING NAME

1.

I am thinking about a client. I don't know his name; he wasn't special. He paid $250 for the hour, just like my other clients, and that's all I really cared about. But he did say this one thing at the end of our sessions. After he had cum and I had washed him off with a warm towel and let him sit in silence for a moment of what I assumed was shame, this client said to me, *Now I feel human again.*

2.

I am thinking of how the quest to find the first human is a cutthroat business. Scientists in Africa fall ill while hunting humanoid fossils, while other scientists in Africa race to discover unrecorded plants before they become extinct due to climate change, while other scientists in Africa supervise the rising statistics of the AIDS pandemic. Paleontologists found Lucy in Ethiopia, though her three-million-year-old femur, right fibula, and right tibia have toured the USA more frequently than Metallica. Lucy may be coming soon to a city near you—have you heard? Her bones neatly labelled and laid in a glass box.

3.

I am thinking of how my community is so keen on labels. I have more ID tags than dollars in my savings account. Queer. Femme. Third-wave feminist. Daddy's-girl-switch-mommy-dom. Clean and sober bar star. Pillow queen. PoMo sexual. Homoflexible. Post-gay gay snot-turned-community revivalist. Art fag. Lit nerd. Whore.

4.

I am thinking the absurdists didn't really believe that nihilism was an appropriate response to life. Rather they were disillusioned playwrights tired of pimping out plot. I am thinking about lost medicine. I am thinking about burned books. I am thinking about starlets with oversized heads: those Powerpuff Girls and Bratz dolls that are doing so well in the marketplace. They wear booty shorts and speak in baby voices but, by god, are they introspective. I mean, their heads are as big as those of the Eight Immortals of Tao. Wow! Workers in China toil up to ninety hours a week to keep up with manufacturing demands—did you know? When asked about these inhumane labour conditions, the spokesman from Walmart had no comment—did you know?

5.

I am thinking about the indigo Navy ship tattooed on my grand-father's arm. As a young man, he lied about his age in order to sign up for the US Navy at seventeen and fight in World War II. His family were WOPs (a term often thought to be an abbreviation for With Out Papers), Italian immigrants who managed to come to America just in time for anti-immigration legislation and the Depression. During his coming-of-age, my grandfather changed his name from Giovanni to John, converted from Catholic to Protestant, and became an illiterate anglophone. He now lives in a trailer park in Florida, filed for bankruptcy last year, and walks with a crippled gait, a limp he's had for as long as I can remember. I think he's finally accepted that I am a homosexual—as long as I continue to look like a lady.

6.

My client—the human—you know, he limped too. I don't know why. I thought it would be a turn-off to ask him what had happened to his leg. It would have been a turn-off to ask him what he knows about vanishing flora or, worse still, vanishing nations. It would have been a turn-off to ask him what will happen to those Chinese factory workers when the Bratz doll craze is over. What would Samuel Beckett say if he knew that Broadway musicals are all that survived of the theatre world? And what would Lucy think if she knew a drunk paleontologist named her after a Beatles song before she was returned to Ethiopia under an international agreement? What would I pay to feel human again?

HEY F*** FACE

1.

Let's be honest. The truth is, I never meant to become an adult fetish worker. I was twenty-four years old, a masseuse at Sensual Bliss Massage & More, on my knees fixing to give a routine blowjob to a man named Stan. Stanley said he had something for me. Something in his briefcase. He shyly produced a pair of handcuffs, a bottle of Tabasco sauce, and a rubber mask that looked like Larry Fine from the Three Stooges. That's how it really began.

2.

As a child, I mistook Larry Fine's fantastic recessive hairline for a monk's tonsure haircut. All Three Stooges looked like clergymen to me. Their absurd speech, I had deduced, was God's punishment for breaking their vows of silence. "Jews can't be monks," my mother informed me. And because I knew everything at age six, I answered, "Oh, yes they can." Women supposedly can't be monks either. But I know my *Lives of the Saints* pretty darn well and, yes, there were F to M—that is Female to Monk—Christian clergy. There was even an F to P—Female to Pope. *La Papessa* reigned for two years, four months, and eight days. This all sounds deliciously renegade, but the truth is, gender-bending clergy were stoned or dragged to death by horses. Even a calling from God won't save us freaks from harm.

3.

Before Frank Zappa had his way with the word "freak," it was principally used as a medical term. Since the early seventeenth century, science has struggled to understand freaks of nature and to classify all kinds of "human congenital malformations" into a system of dysmorphology. A collection of syphilis-ravaged bones, dwarf skeletons, wet specimens of stillborn conjoined twins, and a colon the size of a four-year-old child have been acquired by the Mütter Museum in Philadelphia. The museum's upstairs landing serves as the infamous Soap Lady's grave. A chemical reaction transformed her into a substance like lye. Forensic archaeology tells us that she died before the age of forty, though she's been a specimen for 130 years. I've been there. The place reeks of formaldehyde and is—let's be honest—a less-than-peaceful last resting place.

4.

Not much is known about the Soap Lady's life, but the others—the conjoined twins, the people with extra limbs, the little people—they mostly worked for side shows, circuses, in theatre, or in brothels, like I did. This may sound dismally renegade, but the truth is, the money was great, and greater still was the way the brothel hid me from the world. All the windows were painted black. The day I stuffed my head into that Larry mask, my body became so clandestine that even I didn't know its secrets anymore. Nothing to see through the cut-out eye holes, just peeping circles of Stan's pale skin, the candles' weary glow. If only I could have made a living doing that.

DREAM MAKEOVER

It happened suddenly. It happened without warning. One day I woke up, and I was an old ho.

Before I go on, let's say there are two kinds of hos. The turn-outs are girls in their early twenties or younger who pull into the massage parlour parking lot, late for their shift, in their dented sports coupes with non-fat triple caramel macchiatos in one hand while texting their turn-out girlfriends with the other. Then there are old hos, like me, pushing thirty. Old hos knit booties for their next baby, read distance-ed. textbooks, and braid one another's hair weaves between clients.

Turn-outs sleep off their martini-and-ecstasy hangovers in the staff room. They doze off in impossible positions: their young necks kinked over a sofa's arm, their scrawny legs akimbo.

That used to be me. The only thing that could wake me up was the parlour doorbell. The very second a client came through the door, I'd tumble out of slumber, wander half-asleep into the lobby, and line up beside the other girls for hire. "Hi, my name is Donna," I'd yawn. Clients didn't mind how bed-headed and bleary-eyed I was; they still chose me. I remember the way the old hos sneered as I counted my makes at the end of the night.

It is the duty of an old ho to keep turn-outs in line. I knew I was passing my prime when I caught myself saying things like, "Lexi, you know you can't wear a track suit to work. I don't care if it's Baby Phat by Kimora Lee Simmons. Go put your dress on, girl. This here is a business."

Old hos have scars. We tell war stories that make the turn-outs wince and shudder. We're superstitious. Goodness knows I've slipped a little money under the parlour welcome mat as a good-luck offering.

But the greatest sign of aging is when an old ho begins to quietly reflect upon on her vocation: the hard times, the high times, and most of all, what did I do with all that money?

This happened to me in 2004. I'm pretty sure it was 2004 because the *Ricki Lake Show* had just gone into rerun. Daytime television is the quintessential mirror image of massage parlours. Talk show topics such as "Who is the Baby Daddy?" and "Surprise, Honey, I'm Really a Lesbian!" are bigger components of ho lifestyle than blowjobs. Confounded by these shows, we are perpetually rattled by and relating to the transsexuals and teen mothers and outcasts they sensationalize.

I became fully conscious of my old-ho status while watching an episode called, "You Dissed Me, But Look at Me Now: Today's Guests Are Former Geeks Who Have Become Chic." Before bringing out her guests, Ricki Lake mocked oversized "before" photos of the unfortunate-looking youngsters before they "became chic." Evidently, chic is synonymous with slutty. Braces were replaced by boob jobs and coke-bottle glasses turned in for manes of bleach-blonde hair. Guests flapped around the studio set in outfits skimpier than my work lingerie, hell-bent on proving they were no longer losers.

I'll let you in on a secret. My own grade-school pictures are as awkward as those on the *Ricki Lake Show*: ill-fitting corduroy hand-me-downs and bowl-cut hair. This was almost okay when I was six years old. By junior high, my Sally Ann finds loudly clashed with the polo shirts and penny loafers worn by the other kids. I was also oddly quiet and often stared at other girls. In grade seven, my classmates scratched the words "loser" and "pervert" across my locker. In grade eight, bubble gum was stuck over my face in the class photo that hung in the assembly room. The truth is, I put it there. Even I didn't want to see my own face; it was easier being a wad of pink sticky gum than my own teenage self.

I imagined morphing beneath the bubble gum like a butterfly in a cocoon. One day, I'd peel it off, and underneath I'd have the same spiral perm and diamond stud earrings as the popular girls. I grew up in the age of the makeover movie, the meek-shall-inherit-the-prom flick. These films taught me that if I just hung in there long enough, eventually a cheerleader would take pity on me and teach me how to do my makeup, or a rich preppie would lose a bet and have to take me to the spring dance, or I'd discover that I was actually a teenage werewolf who, even at five feet two inches tall, was awesome at basketball, and all the girls would want to have sex with me.

I clung to the makeover dream for years. My dream shifted from high school sweetheart to winning big at the ho game. Maybe some dumb regular would buy me a condo, or I'd land that mad-money stint in Vegas. My "real life" certainly didn't have any bling makeover potential. I was a poet, a homo with a weakness for broke-ass butch dykes, and I danced burlesque—badly. I ought to have tattooed the word 'penniless' on my titties and tossed in the towel. If I was ever going to go from geek to chic, from trash to cash, I figured ho-ing was the only way. I constantly scanned the adult help-wanted ads for the perfect gig. I chatted online for hours with potential sugar daddies. But even in my final days of sex work, I still hadn't discovered the place where the money was greener.

"Get out of that damn rub and tug," my friend Roxanne told me. She was the one working girl I knew who was older than I was—and she was a high-priced call girl. A grand a night was her norm, and she phoned daily to tell me so. Roxanne had a much higher work ethic than I did too. Her clients were B-list actors who wanted to drum her face with their Viagra erections while she recited the lyrics to "The Wreck of the Edmund Fitzgerald." (No shit.) Whenever her clients requested two girls, I accompanied Roxanne on these calls; each time I sped back to the parlour with a newfound appreciation for the unassuming men flopped atop the massage table.

"Come on. It's not as if you can turn down the cash," Roxanne would start whining before I had a chance to refuse. "Please." She did have a pretty "please." By all accounts, a duo date with Roxanne should have been one of those rare times when I was turned on at work. Roxanne is so tiny she made me feel like a daddy when I'd sit her on my lap. A wry smoker's laugh frequents her pouty lips. And she fucks women.

But, oh no, why be attracted to a cute bisexual when I can develop crushes on the worst homophobes at the massage parlour? The hos that made me hot had fistfuls of gold rings and names like Champagne and Brooklyn. These girls would knock you flat for no good reason. I'd been caught ogling these girls from the corner of my eye. They were never flattered: "What up with the side-eye, bitch? You wanna throw down somethin'?" they'd threaten. *Yes. Yes, I do. I want to throw it down with you right now*, I'd think, as I daydreamed of parting their boot-clad legs. Years after high school, I was being bullied for staring at girls.

When Roxanne was naked, my brain filled with things like when to book my Pomeranian's appointment at the doggie salon or what vegetables might be ready to rot in my fridge. Her clients always wanted to watch us fuck, and we went about it like models at a cheesy portrait studio. We simply posed in front of a backdrop of an orange sunset and pretended to be in Hawaii.

So when Roxanne wanted me to see a woman client with her, I questioned just how much faking it I was capable of. "There is no saying no," snapped Roxanne, her voice loud and delirious. "This is a once-in-a-mother-fucking-lifetime date. The client is fame-o-us."

What Hollywood North star sightings had I recently read about in the newspaper? Maybe the X-Men sequel was still being shot. "Is it Halle Berry?" I guessed.

"Nope," said Roxanne.

"Pamela Anderson is visiting her hometown?"

"Not even close."

"One of the *L-Word* cast wants to find out what lesbian sex is really like?"

Roxanne clicked her tongue to notify me that she was done with my futile guesses.

Even after we arrived at the downtown Sheraton, after we slipped past the chintz-furnished lobby and followed a bellhop up the security-locked elevator, even as we knocked on room number 1608, I had no idea.

Then she opened the door.

She opened the door and suddenly a soundtrack was playing "The Power of Love" by Huey Lewis and the News, The Proclaimers' "500 Miles," songs by Psychedelic Furs, Simple Minds, Echo and the Bunnymen, The Jesus and Mary Chain, old sitcom theme-songs, high school dance songs, slumber party songs—all mashed up into one deafening noise. My entire pubescent life passed before my eyes. I had to blink, breathe, and pull myself together before I could look this client in the face.

Where had this late-1980s/early-1990s actress been for the last decade? Cameo-ing in box-office flops I'd never seen? Tucked away in a quaint Swedish village? Rehab? Her once new-wave hair had grown and hung resignedly around her shoulders. No tiara or neon belt or slouch socks adorned her body. She wore a white robe. Not the hotel robe, mind you, this was silk and clung to the rounded hips I didn't remember her having in the movies.

I decided, then and there, that she had come out of hiding for me. She was a good omen, a gold mine, a sip from the fountain of my youth. Had my makeover moment finally arrived?

Sadly, my greeting came out sounding like a cat being stepped on. The actress handed me our pay in an unsealed envelope, a classy move that I spoiled by holding it upside down so that the stack of hundred dollar bills slipped out and scattered across the carpet. I then hit my head on the cherry wood vanity as I knelt to retrieve the money.

It was up to Roxanne to infuse any sex appeal into the situation. She miraculously produced a tangerine-vanilla-scented candle and a bottle of Merlot from her purse. Roxanne made me proud to be an old ho.

I remained jaw-dropped and useless, until a certain silk robe was tossed over the upholstered headboard and the actress lay naked on the bed. I held my breath as I crawled beside this celluloid queen. Her skin did a fine job of imitating the discarded robe. On her, each wrinkle was as crafted as embroidery on silk. I had never seen nipples so pink. They were like the "you are here" dots on a map. When I touched her, she sighed the kind of sigh only someone who's had vocal coaching could make, like a tuning fork lived in her throat. Her thighs twitched as I arrived at her clit. I wanted to freeze-frame and study her for a while, but Roxanne had my hand bagged and lubricated faster than I can say "finger bang." We were hos on a clock. Roxanne was wide-eyed and grave, as if wordlessly urging me to make haste. Go bravely forward.

So I did.

As I toyed with the actress's clit, I saw that hardened wad of bubble gum stuck to my grade-eight class photo coming loose. Sliding inside her was like sliding into my past. Not my awkward loser past, but the past I always dreamed of.

I was fucking the prom queen, the rebel girl, the cheerleader, and the school slut—all at the same time. I made her wriggle and kick. Her head lurched atop the pillow. I wondered if she'd squirt or ooze when she came. If she'd scream or if she'd swear. Would a parade of 1987 Chevy El Caminos race down the street below? Would all the mirrored disco balls in the whole city start spinning? Somewhere a cheerleader would wave her pompoms high—"Gimmie a C. Gimmie a U. Gimmie an M."

I mused over this pending orgasm for a quite a while before I noticed that the actress wasn't having one. My arm was growing tired. I looked over at Roxanne as she thrummed the client's nipples in a drum-roll of anticipation. "Oh yeah. That's right," she said, urging the actress to finish. Her tone was the same she took with all the men—a put-on sultry, one that thinly disguised her impatience.

The actress's A-note sighs turned to dog-like whimpers. Her brow furrowed. I suspected that if she was going to get off, the moment had already passed, but still I kept fucking her. Roxanne eyed the time on her watch, and still I kept fucking. I heard the tiny bones in my wrist creaking. I kept fucking. A turn-out would have given up and handed the client a vibrator, but I kept on fucking.

The white robe trembled on the clacking headboard like an old ghost, still haunting me. I understood very clearly then that there would be no cumload of cash or fame. No *Ricki Lake Show*. No free condos. No Viva Las Vegas. I could fuck and fuck and still never satisfy the makeover dream. The bubblegum had already been removed, and I knew that this is what I am: a queer femme who often has misguided crushes, dances low-rent burlesque in sticky-floored dyke bars, and writes goddamn poetry.

And what, I asked myself as I pulled out of the famous actress's pussy, is wrong with that?

SENSUAL BLISS MASSAGE & MORE

There are no windows in this house.
The candle flame and the calla lily
quickly die. Never ask a withered leaf to tell its story.

Weary skin gathers around each knuckle. Swollen
fingertip. Shallow vein. A withered leaf turns
to embroidered silk in these hands.

In his hands is your sugar cake your story
book your silver coin. In his hands
is the heartache that reminds him of you.

In your hands is the wine glass about to break.
Salute, friend. He leaves as you are picking shards
from the floor.

The wine bottle has been passed around the room.
We sang the same song in rounds all night.
Why is it you still don't know my name?

Look further than the ache of each approaching fingertip.
Think back to that collage of clouds.
Somewhere a sparrow slips through the fragile sky.

How will these stories be carried from your tongue
without the wind? Handle each word like a fallen bird
for there are no windows in this house.

YOU ARE HERE (A MAP)

Here the vase on the night table is an empty cocktail glass, without
the brown daffodils in the wastebasket, waiting to be filled
with a new doomed beauty.

Red lips speak for themselves. Here is a place where your body
is the protagonist,
no partner,
no significant other, divorced from the heart.

All the hanging pictures are of water-coloured flowers. Roses,
lilies, daffodils are quiet fires
in a cool green meadow whispering,
Cut me. You don't have to know me. I'm easily replaced.

In each room there is a man who says he is lost. You raise his ghost
from the grave.
Later, his ghost is crumpled
in a tissue, washed away with anti-bacterial soap, his thumbprint

on a hundred-dollar bill. Here memory is as lasting as the images
in the bed's mirrored headboard. In each room
there is a man who says he is lost.

Tonight your hands are named exile and limbo.
Your voice sounds like the air inside a vase.
If the neon sign above the entrance burned out,
would you know where you are?

HOW TO BURY OUR DEAD
for Shelby Tom

Have you ever had to attend a Catholic or Sikh or Japanese or Irish funeral and felt a little uncertain about the cultural grieving practices? We can all thank cyberspace for easy-to-find funeral etiquette. Simply visit Wikipedia before you do something tactless, like sending flowers to a Jewish funeral service.

Now try doing a search for "queer funeral etiquette"; Wikipedia will tell you that "The page 'Queer funeral etiquette' does not exist." Now try Googling it. When I first tried this, the closest result was a website that explained tipping etiquette for gay men vacationing in Mexico. There are now a few online discussions.

It only got worse when I swapped labels and mixed up words. The first result on a search for "gay memorial service" brought me to an article about a Navy veteran's funeral that was cancelled when his church congregation learned that he was gay. If you search for this story, you will discover that this happened in 2007.

Everyone dies; we can agree on that. And although we probably don't really like to, we can also agree that the mortality rate for queers is higher than for heterosexuals. Doesn't it seem a little off that we—with our rich array of community rituals and traditions—don't have customs for mourning? Exactly how do we bury our dead?

I am not an expert. All of my grieving has been done in rather bitter privacy. I can only share with you my own stories of bereavement in the hope that they help spark conversation, and that conversation brings change. I believe this is the way we queer folks do things.

I'll start with what I know: My family is made up of mostly

hard-working farmers, churchgoers, and people who strongly believe in heaven. I was seven years old when I attended my first funeral. My great-uncle Dave lived with his wife Dottie on a corn and chicken farm until he died of a heart attack before the age of fifty. My ma made a bed for me in the back seat of our Volkswagen Rabbit and drove without stopping from Fort Erie, Ontario, to Auburn, New York. Her good black dress hung in the back passenger-side window, a funeral-garb curtain that blocked the sun as I dozed away the five-hour drive.

When we arrived, Dave and Dottie's frame house was still as huge and white as ever. The corn still stood in dutiful rows. Willow trees sprawled across the front lawn, still waiting for grandkids and cousins to climb them. Dottie's mean-tempered geese chased me up the driveway, hissing, like they always had done.

Ma led me to the back door—because family never came through the front—and into the mudroom where Uncle Dave's flannel shirts crowded the coat tree. I watched her gulp back a grief-stricken sob as she searched for an empty hook for my red wool poncho. While being raised by a single mom, I had seen plenty of tears. Ma wasn't one to hide her most recent dating disaster or debt struggles, but this was different. This sounded as if something had been dislodged from deep within her body. Her crying fired up loudly and continued, almost mechanically, as we were received by a half-dozen or so aunties and passed around the kitchen from one set of open arms to the next.

What I learned about funerals that day: You get to keep your (Sunday) shoes on inside the house. Cake and pie arrive in landslides. No one jabbers when the priest stays to drink with the family. Well-recited stories are told about when the departed either comically injured or humiliated themselves or both. You cry whenever the crying comes. Maybe it's when your second cousin, Holly, hugs you so tight and uncomfortably long that you feel her faux-pearl necklace denting your forehead. Maybe it's when you're in the living room, where the open casket lies for three days, forcing yourself to look at the pale and gentle flesh of your uncle's closed eyelids. When you cry, it's uncensored. And you're not alone.

It's likely that we all have a story something like this: a memory of bagpipes or a parade of black suits or of kneeling for so long that your feet fall asleep. I wonder if our memories could be the key to shaping queer funerals? Conquering and compiling the fine details—the unearthly quiet of a receiving room or how particularly buttery the sweets tasted. Or, in my case, how much the tattooist's gun burned on my back.

I mourned my first queer death in a tattoo shop. There's a scarlet-haired, rock-n-roll vixen on my back. She peeks out of my shirt collar and runs, right beside my spine, down toward my hips. I clenched my fists (and my jaw and my butt cheeks) for nearly eight hours before the tattooist was finished.

She attracts a lot of attention, my tattoo. Especially from biker types who don't have any qualms about touching a perfect stranger's back. "Nice ink," they say. Some have even gone as far as to slide my tank top to the side to get a better look. So when they ask, "What made you get that?" I feel a certain vindication when I tell them, "It's a memorial tattoo for a lover. She was nineteen when she died."

The conversation usually ends there.

If I were to continue, I'd say I picked up a phone call from a friend sometime in the late fall of 1993. This friend and I hadn't spoken since high school, and she didn't waste words asking how I was doing all the way out in Vancouver. Her news was swift as a kick: Val overdosed in her parents' rec room. The "immediate-family-only" service had already passed. Her obituary had already run in the Niagara-area local papers.

"But I didn't even know she moved home," was the only response I could come up with. It was true, it must have been at least a year since I had seen her.

"Well," my friend sighed, sounding impatient. "She came back to get clean."

The last place I had seen Val was at my old dealer's house, so that is where I went to announce Val's death. Some people there lay unmoving on the many ragged sofas jammed into the tiny apartment and slept through the news. Some had never met Val and shrugged in careless sympathy. I stuck around for the three or four people who had called Val a friend—despite the fact that the second-hand freebase coke smoke was making me both ill and filled with cravings.

We told stories: Remember how we used to cut class to swim in the Gorge? Remember tobogganing on garbage-bag sleds at Sugar Bowl Park? Remember Black Label beer and our secret drinking spot near Devil's Hole? How'd we manage not to kill ourselves when climbing drunk down to those caves?

After we'd exhausted the tales from high school, the road-trip sagas began: Val could neither read a map nor stay awake at the wheel, but she could always find a radio station, even in the butt-fuck-nowhere prairies where nothing but tall grass lives.

From these stories I omitted the part when Val tucked my hands under her bomber jacket and held them against her bare belly until my fingers were warm in the November night. Our first kiss took place after we had ducked between two parked cars in a bowling alley parking lot. I used to chew my lips raw daydreaming about when we'd kiss again. I noticed things about her that made me light-headed and confused: She always wore such short skirts that if she sat on a vinyl chair, she'd leave a faint sweat imprint of her thighs. I struck these tales from our impromptu memorial because Val and I were the only ones who knew about them. Now that she was dead, I was the only one.

The lack of "out" funerals has been going on long before I lost a loved one. In 1987 Cleve Jones and a group of San Franciscan LGBT activists began the AIDS Memorial Quilt, an enormous and ever-growing homage to the lives of people who died of AIDS-related causes. In the late 1980s most of the people who died with AIDS—the gay men who died with AIDS—were denied memorial services because funeral homes and cemeteries refused to take their remains. The Quilt was one of the only places where surviving loved ones could formally remember and grieve.

If you visit *aidsquilt.org*, you'll notice that the NAMES Project Foundation has honourably chosen to use the site as an educational tool and an affirming celebration of life. Click the "Make a Panel" button and read the encouraging guidelines on to how to submit your own panel to the quilt. Anything from hand-embroidery to spray paint art is welcome. The only specific requirement is the dimensions: six feet by three feet. This is the size of a human grave, a nod back to the times when we had to bury our dead in cloth coffins we made ourselves.

As a kinky, genderqueer femme with a big mouth and what you could call a rather enterprising pussy, I am accustomed to having to create my own family, my home and community, and even myself. I am proud of the keen ability queer folks have to create personal, joyful somethings out of the nothings we're all too often offered. I don't know, however, if I can be proud that we've had to make our own coffins.

After the tattoo shop, I grieved in gay bar bathrooms, a New Orleans-bound van full of travelling burlesque dancers, and a massage-parlour staff room. This may sound bad ass—but really, where else can we hold queer services? Annual memorials and days of remembrance have been an answer to this. Often housed at progressive university campuses or hosted by social justice groups, these mass memorials allow us to remember our own. At least, they try to.

In spring 2003, I was working at a garishly decorated "rub-n-tug" next to the King George Highway. It was a bad month for business, and some girls started working double shifts or hitting the stroll on Richards Street after the massage parlour closed for the night to keep from going broke. At times like this, I was thankful to be a penniless homosexual artist who could live happily on a couple of weekly dates with regular clients.

Whenever business was slow, the staff inevitably grew louder. We perfected our booty shake to blaring hip-hop, smoked marijuana until we broke into giggle fits, and killed hours bitching on the phone to other working girls at other massage parlours about how business was slow. So when I showed up to a dead-silent workplace one day in May, I knew something was wrong. I walked down the vacant hallway, past the row of empty massage studios to the staff room where I found Summer looking crumpled, with her head in her hands. The other girls stared at the floor. Summer was no crybaby; a high school drop out and single mom, her baby's daddy was murdered, and her boyfriend was in prison up north.

"Who died?" I asked, gravely.

"Shelby, fuck. You remember Shelby. Chinese. Tranny. Worked by the name of Ling. You know, that older Asian girl."

Tranny was Summer's way of saying that Shelby was a trans woman who worked the streets. I did remember her. She worked downtown alongside the high-track, big-money girls. Summer said the word on Shelby was that she had been cut into pieces and left in a shopping cart outside a laundromat.

During the days that followed, we watched the local news and brought the papers to work. We didn't hear anything about Shelby; no obituary and no funeral—it was as if Shelby had never existed. I was left to wonder how it happened. I couldn't help but think that Shelby was targeted because of gender. Gender, race, and occupation, I was certain, were the reasons for the lack of media coverage. After about a week, we decided to light a candle and say a prayer in the staff room and move on.

Six months later, I was given a flyer for the Transgender Day of Remembrance. Each year on November 20, the transgender people across North America and the world who have died are remembered. Many cites have observed the Transgender Day of Remembrance since 1999. Over the years, it has grown from small DIY gatherings to well-publicized and attended events. I wondered if Shelby would be among those being remembered: I prayed that she would be.

I invited Summer to come with me and mourn. She eyed the memorial's flyer, with its activist jargon, and saw that it was being held at a university campus. "Not my thing," she said and handed the flyer back to me.

I went alone. As I entered the crowded campus classroom, my chest tightened. There were many familiar faces: college queers, forefathers and mothers of local trans activism; there was even a Member of Parliament. More people than seats, so they stood along the back wall and crouched in front of the speaker's table. Seeing them all suddenly made Shelby's death more real. Overwhelmed, I squatted on the newly carpeted floor, close to the exit.

I had a short eulogy that I wanted to share. I wanted to let people know that Shelby was a strong woman. With all respect, she was a tough-ass bitch. From what I knew of her, she never hid or compromised who she was. It couldn't have been easy working alongside pimps and rows of nineteen-year-old girls for hire. She often played a mommy-role on the stroll—helping girls rather than competing with them. I also wanted to invite anyone in the room who knew Shelby to share a story or two.

I did not get an opportunity to say any of this. The memorial quickly turned into a political meeting, a soundboard for topics such as surgery funding, the recently disbanded gender clinic, and trans inclusion in the Bill of Human Rights. A short documentary about San Francisco's Day of Remembrance was screened. I remember growing anxious at about this time; I watched one of the speakers struggle with the borrowed film projector and began to wonder when we were going to read the names. When were we going to remember our dead?

I was visibly fidgeting when the list of names was finally brought out and passed around. Each person present took one name from the list. One by one, the names of the deceased and circumstances of their deaths were read out loud—mostly women's names and mostly violent deaths. I heard someone say, "My name is Shelby Tom, I worked as a prostitute in Vancouver, Canada. I was forty years old when I was murdered, allegedly by a client. My body was found in a shopping cart in North Vancouver."

A loud wail escaped my lips, and I buried my head into my legs to prevent more from coming out. No one else was crying out loud, so I figured the appropriate thing to do was keep my head down until I felt my jeans grow damp with tears. I was still crying when an abrupt announcement was made that time had run out, the university was closing, and we needed to leave.

Campus security ushered us out of the building. I moved along in a slow, dizzy line as people looked at me with pity. A woman asked me if I'd be all right. I believe she had a soft-butch haircut and a bike helmet and maybe even was someone I knew. When she hugged me, I held my breath, determined not to cry all over her. I was embarrassed of my uncontainable and seemingly unshared display of emotion. I have not since been to a Transgender Day of Remembrance.

Make two lists, one of queers you know who have died, and a second of queer funerals you've attended. How do your lists compare? My first list is a whole lot longer than the second. What I've learned about queer funerals is—they don't exist. In the worst-case scenario, we are forced back into the closet at our funerals. At best, our deaths become political platforms for public education and human rights lobbying. They become measures of the work that still needs to be done in this world. I am proud to be a part of a community that, in the face of death, rolls up its sleeves and says, *We've got a job to do.* At the same time, at risk of sounding enfeebled, it's just not fair. How truly sad it is to not be afforded a funeral!

So I have no expert advice on "how to bury your dead" because I've never actually done so. But that doesn't mean I haven't imagined an old country farmhouse filled with queer folk who have gathered to properly grieve. Maybe you can imagine it too. Picture Mac jackets and faux-fur and good leather hung in the mudroom. You come in through the back door because family never comes through the front, and you are family. You can hold your partner's hand the whole time, until your fingers grow numb, if you want to. The stories shared here are uncensored, including the ones that take place in bathroom stalls or parked cars. Photos, taken at Pride Parade or Faerie Camp or the bar, make their rounds around the room. When you are handed the photo of yourself—you with the loved one you came to mourn—stare down at it until the colours start to blur and you find yourself whispering, "Thank you, thank you, thank you."

And when you're ready, go bravely into the living room where the casket lies. Take as long as you need; this moment is yours to say goodbye. Imagine this last look. Imagine hair and hands, eyelashes and lower lip, and all the memories that a body holds to it.

Our lives are worth the fruit baskets and raisin cakes. We are worth calla lilies and pink roses. We're worth stone markers or scattered ashes. Hymn and song. Wine and ritual. Surely we've all earned hours of storytelling. And most certainly, our lives are worth the tears.

SCULPTED FROM LIGHT

won't you celebrate with me
what I have shaped into
a kind of life? I had no model.
born in babylon
—Lucille Clifton, "won't you celebrate with me"

Your body tells a story
if you look.
This curled scar along my right arm
was once a cradle.
rocked me rocked   me
Outside the nursery window a May
pole, Dionysus' frenzied dance,
opium smoke, my mother
a Sabine woman, raped.
Born in Babylon

my baby teeth grew only
to chew the flesh of another,
bite mark: crescent moon,
cupid's bow on my own
skin. What I learned
about lips and limb, pussy
and heart: unmentionable.
Is desecration teaching?
Is violence knowledge? Is haunting
a kind of life? I had no model
for rebirth. No second coming blueprint.

True, Hokusai painted the phoenix,
Raphael, Christ's ascension.
There were neither gods nor painters laid in my tomb
only the slow process of the body.
Never mind past lives never mind elixir
of eternal youth dragon's breath never
mind the Elysian fields transcendent
wisdom never mind orchid.
What I have shaped into

self is very small, only
a buttercup's pistil,
or a single blade of grass and today
I did not bend in the wind, today
a ladybug tiptoed along my spine.
Place your hand
in front of the sun,
slivers of light shine through.
Hold it. It is your light now.
Won't you come celebrate with me.

MISSING CHILDREN

i am going back to find the body.
where was it i left it—
robed in scarlet in a church window,
in the neighbour's pear tree, juice from torn skins
—Beth Goobie, "creed"

Age is an agreement of economics, a lesson
in having less. How small is painless?
I afford myself limited space: the tip of a knife
cutting the white seam of cartilage from meat. How blood
enters the open pores of the chopping board is not important.
The only question now: when can I eat? Hunger,
before it became just another desire to quell, would devour
everything. Bit into sky, licked landscape like fire, killed
wild buffalo, sucked marrow from bone, thrashed
in a neighbour's pear tree, juice from torn skins ran

toward the Atlantic where ships' sails were once filled
with my own breath. A quest. New lands
discovered. A four-hundred-million-year-old mountain
given a new name. *I survived*
the first winter and then the plague's ecumenical heat;
the dead buried before growing cold. There was a bed
of nails to sleep on and live coal to walk across.
Whores were burned, virgins turned to stone.
Who knows for certain if I wasn't the child
robed in scarlet in a church window.

Who can say how long lamps will stay lit,
what verse is abandoned in ash, what song
lures us too far into the forest
what heat curls our newfound wings.
Infinite mystery inhabits a young body. Skulls
are ceilings painted with the heavens.
Timeline, like gold thread, woven into skins.
It took years to map and chart these lands,
much was lost along the way
where was it i left it—

my pansophic tongue, my phantasmic eye?
How long have I been without them?
Age has estranged me from my motherland; artifacts sold
to private collections, hidden treasure more deeply hidden.
Come close and listen—new emotion is dear, my friend,
you must learn to survive on memory.
Let it whisper in your ear, let it take up your hand,
without food or rest it travels.
Let memory lead you home again.
i am going back to find *my body.*

HOW I GOT MY TATTOO

Every other weekend I ate green olives, crude slices of cheddar,
Ritz crackers, smoked sardines straight from the can
with the turn-key lid, garlic pickles, and pepperoni dipped in sour
cream, spring onions, and hard-boiled eggs rolled under my father

's palm until the shell fell away like lizard skins then rolled again
in a mound of kosher salt because these were the foods
that coalesced with father's recent divorce status
and with beer. When

I hit my girlfriend, Valentine, with the phone receiver (a decade
later) I was dead set on having olives as the complimentary topping
on our delivery pizza. She wanted green peppers and bellyached

about how we never ate vegetables and we'd stopped
going for our all-night walks. We only walked those walks,
I reminded her, for the city to become field, or empty
parking lot, or a stretch of quiet railroad where we could kiss
each other raw and scream and hide
from Burgard Vocational High School and god and

daylight. Cocaine
is turning you into a fucking asshole, she said and picked olives
from her half of the pizza to feed them to me, a few missed
my mouth and rolled inside my shirt then onto the gold and denim
blue floral sofa, where we slept, a mess
of limbs and unconscious youth. I never lost my appetite

as an addict. I'm glad I was a girl and there were horse races
and truck stops and twenty-four hour diners where a girl,
with a bit of glitter lip gloss, could count on
the done-with-their-day men, up-or-down-on-their-luck men,
ball-busted broken-backed men, plain-sick-of-spending-time-
with-other-men men to offer a grilled cheese sandwich and a bit
of pocket money
so I didn't have to raid the dumpster

behind the Nabisco factory with Petey and Steve.
They always smelled like corn syrup. Petey had beautiful eyelashes
that hid the bloodshot like a burlesque dancer
's feather fans. I would have let him touch me but his hands were
the kind of filthy that won't scrub clean.
I wish I could say I've been clean

since the day Valentine died. I was living in an artist loft
where I made non-wearable ball gowns out of copper wire,
old costume jewellery, and crayfish
claws I had saved up over the years and spray painted gold.
My girlfriend at the time, Jesse, was kind and always lied
when I asked her if my art stank like fish, she had her arms around
me before I even hung up the phone. Valentine's little sister told me
I was the only one she would call, me and 911.

I returned to my old dealer's house with the Confederate flag hung
in the bay window and the stupid smoke that couldn't find
its way out of the living room and I told everyone there
Valentine had overdosed in her sister's bathroom and the funeral
was on a Wednesday at Our Lady of Perpetual Forgiveness Church.
My skin itched
from the second-hand freebased coke
and I had to go home and take seventeen
Gravol because that is all we had in the medicine cabinet
and I wanted to sleep
for as many days as humanly possible
but Jesse made me walk
in circles around the coffee
table for hours
before she was sure
I wouldn't pass out cold.
I quit

for good up North in a small village where my hosts brought down
a deer which I volunteered to help them skin and piece the meat.
I didn't expect the animal to resist the knife the way it did.
Everyone was amused at how I struggled
with its heavy leg in my lace-trimmed summer dress, they said
they had never seen a white girl so willing
to get blood on her hands since their land was taken.
The children made up words
and told me they were First Peoples' words,
then laughed hysterically
when I tried to repeat these words back to them. I guess,
without realizing it,

I escaped by becoming an outsider. Sure, I've travelled
and gotten the kind of attention a girl gets when she is travelling
alone. The tattoo
on my back has been a means for men
and women to initiate conversation or touch, poking at the raised
ink peeking out of my shirt collar.
Junko approached me in a park

in Osaka while I was trying to coax a stray dog to let me pet it, and
asked me to come
for karaoke and drinks. I ordered cream soda that surprised me
by being emerald green.
The cartoonish rendition of Valentine, her half
-winking eye, her leopard-print swimsuit,
her halo that was supposed to be gold but I got too sore
for the tattooist to finish the colour made Junko ask,
why did you get this tattoo

I told her to kiss Valentine's lips: my shoulder. We sang Beatles'
songs: "I feel the ice is slowly melting, little darling,
it seems like years since it's been clear."

LYING IS THE WORK

"How old are you?" he asks as he opens the door.

There is no right answer to this question, so I guess. "Twenty-seven."

"Becky told me you were twenty-five."

Becky isn't a real woman. She is the name that all three of the receptionists at the escort agency use when arranging outcalls. Becky's job is to move product. The product is sexual fantasy, which differs from other products in that the buyer wants to be an uninformed consumer. In this marketplace of attractive inaccuracy, if the client on the phone likes breasts, Becky makes double Ds out of C-cups. If he likes younger women, Becky tells him I am twenty-five.

As the worker—the sex worker—the job is less about embodying the client's fantasy and more about making the imitation seem like money well spent. Lying about my age, breast size, weight, cultural background, hair colour, college education, lust for certain sex acts and so on, is a routine guile that routinely causes me anxiety. Where will the client draw the line between fantasy and deception? The fantasy holds my payment. But finding myself on the side of deception is delicate. Let's just say that in sex work, there is no standardized way for a client to lodge a complaint.

Standing rigid and at least six feet tall in the threshold of his waterfront home, this man begrudgingly decides it is worth $250 to pretend that I am twenty-five, when actually I am thirty. He hands me a billfold and ushers me in.

✦

My grandfather once lied about his age. He lied in order to sign up with the Navy at the age of seventeen and fight in World War II.

His parents were Casertani Italians who managed to come to the United States in the wake of the Immigration Act of 1924—an act proposed by eugenicist congressmen and nearly unanimously approved by the Senate. Its aim was to limit the number of immigrants of "inferior stock." Before he reached his teens, my grandfather was given an Anglo-Saxon name (John), along with the scores of Vincenzos who become Vincents, Guerinos who become Warrens, and Perlitas who become Pearls. Italian was no longer spoken in their home; it became a forbidden language outside of the home, and eventually English dominated their dinner table too. As my grandfather reached what would have been his senior year of high school, Italian-Americans were being arrested, sent to internment camps, or issued enemy-alien registration cards. He, however, carried out his all-American assimilation by shipping out to war. He spent "too long," he said, anchored in the East China Sea.

"Too long" is one of the few things I've heard him say directly about his life as a soldier. He has always been a silent gargoyle sitting at the head of our family table. I've pieced together his story from what little my relatives have shared in hushed disclosures and from reading other soldiers' biographies, visiting museums, and watching the documentary channel. I've adopted historic facts collected by experts and academics as my heritage. I've learned about my grandfather the way many of us (Generation Xers) learn about their elders, whose voices have been muted by dissociation, depression, alcoholism, trauma, and denial.

Only his body holds proof: the faded indigo Navy ship tattooed on his left arm. His crippled gait.

✦

"How much do you think I paid for this house?" is his second question. He lives alone in a detached two-storey home with a relatively unobstructed view of Vancouver Harbour. The safest outcall clients are family men whose wives are out for the evening or whose children are off camping. Family men might even include recent divorcees or widowers. Family men are frequently nice, but more importantly, they have something to lose if the adult transaction they're engaging in is anything short of discreet and benign. Family men ask you what you are studying at college. Family men offer apologies without explaining what they are apologizing for.

A framed poster of the Eiffel Tower is the only thing hanging on this client's beige walls. All of his furniture is dark wood, tempered glass, and black leather.

"Close to a million, I'm sure," I answer.

"Mortgage poor," he calls himself. "People assume I have it easy."

We sit with the lights on and curtains wide open, staring out his panoramic living room window. Is he staging a show for his neighbours, I wonder. Will the impending blowjob be witnessed by a senior couple out walking their Bichon Frisé? But he spends the better part of our hour-long session monologuing about the house, his speech punctuated by frequent trips to the washroom. Each time he emerges, he wrings his hands. "Just needed to wash up," he says. His hastened, nasal intonation tells me he is actually doing cocaine. I assume the coke is hampering his erection.

I am preparing to leave when he pulls out another billfold. I want to refuse to extend our session, but Becky already told him I could stay. In fact, Becky offered him a deal on his second hour. This is an atypical course for a client to take. Normally, the client seeks cues from me. If I appear to be enjoying myself, the client might invite me to stay longer, and then I make the call to Becky. For show, I often speak as if I'm gossiping with a girlfriend, giddy with the racy details. *Ohhh, Becky, we're just getting warmed up, if you catch my meaning. Please say I can spend another hour!*

Mr Million-dollar-property doesn't want my routine flirtations. He says, "What? You thought the night was over?" as I force myself to keep smiling. We move downstairs to a windowless spare bedroom, and I notice my cell phone loses its signal. His speech about property taxes is now laced with aloof instructions such as "remove your dress" and "slowly." He paces half-circles around the bed and flexes his muscles in a mirror of his own imagination.

Pity is an emotion I hope to refrain from in daily life, but there are times when a little superiority and compassion help me feel in control with my clients. What does this man have to prove? And to whom, I wonder. He is alone in this house, after all. What hurts have caused him to spend his Saturday night with cocaine and a prostitute whom he clearly distrusts? When he touches me, he goes about it as if I am an animal in a cage. He reaches his arm in, handles my body for a moment, then recoils.

"Sit," I encourage him, patting the bed beside me. "I'll help you relax." My invitation goes unacknowledged. He continues to pace, keeping the tension in the room in motion with his rush-drug strides.

He's only half-undressed when he decides to take another washroom break. I use the opportunity to sneak back up the stairs. I've got my heels on. My hand touches the front doorknob when I realize I left my cell phone in his spare room. If I duck out without it, this client could call all of the people in my phone book and tell them I'm a whore. I consider the potential damages while running through my list of contacts in my head. It's not that I'm ashamed. It's just that this—pardon my language—fuckwad does not deserve the chance to tell my story. He has no right to reach the people I know and love.

I unlock the deadbolt and, using his leather dress boot as a doorstop, leave the door cracked open. The exit is set for a quick escape. I go back downstairs to the windowless spare bedroom.

✦

My dear reader, if only I could talk to you in more than a narrative direct address and break the fourth-wall monologue. I wish this were a two-way conversation. I'd like to ask if you are worried about the female protagonist (me) of this nonfiction story. I'd like to know why you are worried. How big is this worry? Do I (the protagonist) represent something larger than the 3,000-odd words of this story, the 150-odd pages of this book? And what will we (you and I) do about it? We'll get to that, won't we? What can we do with this big "representational" worry?

You see, I came out as a sex worker (among other things) when I was twenty years old, and have been making public statements about sex work ever since. When I began writing about sex work, publishers and reviewers described my voice as "transgressive" and "no-holds-barred." When issues like decriminalization, the kiddie stroll, and missing women catch the public's attention, the media contacts me for quotes. When I am grocery shopping, young women approach me. "I have a friend," they say, "who would really like to meet you. I think you could help them." I'm honoured, but am I honest?

Can honesty sit side-by-side with omission if I'm always telling only part of the story? If omission is lying, then I guess I'm a ____. As a statement-maker and storyteller, I have certain truths that I push forward to demonstrate that sex workers are worthy of esteem, dignity, and sanction. There are also truths that I believe will disgrace and discredit me and render me an unreliable narrator. I don't tell the stories that might make sex workers "look bad." *How Poetry Saved My Life* is my attempt to tell—not confess—a selected few of my truths.

✦

But, for now, here are a few more statements:

Lying is the work of people who are told their truths have no value.

The labour of survival is laden with myth and misunderstanding.

Silence is the work of people who can't comprehend that change is possible.

(I still moonlight at all of these jobs.)

✦

He has removed his clothes and his naked gym-body is laid out on the bed. Even his erection is posing. He sees I have my shoes on in his house—*his house*—and is pissed as hell. The fight escalates quickly, the two of us screaming over each other, neither doing anything to moderate our rage. When the first blow arrives, everything slows into a sloppy choreography of mistimed swings and awkward kicks.

He backs me into a closet. I jut my leg out before the door closes.

✦

My grandfather's legs look like ghosts. They are shrunken from nerve damage, disproportionately small beneath his barrel-chested body. From his hips down, his skin is ashy and pale because of lack of circulation. He used to visit us for Veterans' Day at the Erie County Fairgrounds to gather with the other surviving men of his platoon. His spindly legs deftly carried him along the Memorial Parade runway lined with red, white, and blue paper carnations. At this time of year, Erie County was flat, hot, and fetid with algae blooms and pollution from the lake. The setting empathized with the occasion.

As a child, I had one simple duty during these visits: to keep away from him, especially if he was drinking.

Recently I learned that his disability was not from a combat injury. Some twenty years after the war ended, he crashed his car while driving drunk. His back broke. He was lucky that he didn't become a paraplegic. His passenger—believed to be his mistress— died instantly. This discovery baffled me; I felt I had been misled. The admissible excuse for being such a mean, broken man is war heroics. Fallen soldiers are pathos-worthy and therefore romantic. They are commemorated on collectors' coins.

The Royal Mint does not make an Oppression Is Pervasive coin.

A similar bind exists for sex workers. The admissible excuse for being a low, demoralized woman is survivor heroism. She should have a past tough enough to explain her bad choices. She must spend her earnings on education, not on drugs or so-called frivolous things like clothing or childcare. She should volunteer, write poems, care for an aged parent, or otherwise embrace the romantic "tart with a heart" trope. To avoid appearing like she is trapped, she should exit the sex trade by the age of thirty. A pathos-worthy sex worker must be articulate, not exasperated nor jaded, when telling her story.

While I am well aware of such binds, I admit that it is still more comfortable to believe that my grandfather was injured in the war, because wars end. The idea that the battle has an expiry date is very nice. I'm not impervious to those black-and-white photos of the Welcome Home parade down Broadway. The tickertape haze. Reunited couples kissing in the street. Imagine for a moment carrying a banner that reads, "We Won!"

The signs and banners I've carried while marching in the streets have never read, "We Won!" Nonetheless, I have followed the required steps for survivor heroism. I am an articulate former sex worker who—for the most part—used my earnings for personal advancement. From this privileged position, I have been asked many times how this "prostitution thing" happened to me. Often the question is augmented with what I am meant to take as a compliment: How did this "prostitution thing" happen to such a nice girl/such a smart girl/an exceptional girl/a girl with such potential?

This question makes me "feel bad." So in response, I offer facts collected by experts and academics.

At any given time in Canada, an average of two percent of the female population is working in the sex trade. This is the one industry where women earn more than their male counterparts. Female sex workers can earn more per hour than at any other entry-level job. This gender bias, unique to the sex trade, has provided unwed women with financial security and opportunity since ancient times. The first known record of this occurred in 1800 BCE when the Babylonian King Hammurabi decreed that prostitutes had the right to inheritance, savings, and property. Prostitution is the world's oldest profession, as the saying goes.

More recently, it's been estimated that up to seventy percent of sex workers grew up and continue to live below the national poverty line. Up to eighty-five percent of prostitutes have experienced homelessness. Up to ninety percent of prostitutes were abused as children. The average age to enter prostitution is fourteen. You see? I do represent something much larger than the 150-odd pages in this book.

✦

Through the gap in the closet door, I see his face flushed red and the undecorated beige wall behind him. I see my black stiletto heel is still on my foot. The rest of my body is in the dark.

Slumped feebly inside the closet floor, I am not scared that I will die. The client stomps on my calf and knee, but his beating is somehow indifferent. I get the feeling he would rather that I just disappear altogether. I wait so long for him to tire that I begin to wonder if it feels less cruel to beat a leg than a whole person. Could he half-heartedly hit me in the face for this long? On my end, it feels less painful to be just a leg, and not a whole person.

My dear reader, I have not brought you here to worry about my life. Remember that pity is an emotion that doesn't really get us anywhere. And we (you and I) will get somewhere with this, won't we? Right now, I want to remind you of how this moment represents all of our lives. Part of us is hurting while part of us is unable to see the injury. We must talk more about this disconnect.

It is this disconnect—this lie—that enables me to adopt a brutal tone as I threaten to ruin all the plastic-covered suits in his closet. It allows me to coldly strike him in the face with a clothes hanger and limp out of his house. When I call Becky, she asks me to see one more client for the night, and this disconnect offers me the capacity to agree. "This is my last job. Tomorrow, I'll quit. I mean it, Becky," I say.

I stop at a pharmacy, buy a pair of thigh-high black stockings to cover the cuts and swelling, and go to meet my next client.

Over the following months, I see another two or three dozen clients. I pay rent and tuition, and save up a little "retirement" fund. I make myself remember this bad date and make myself remember again. I tell friends what happened. I write it down. Connecting to this memory—owning it—is much harder than living through it, but I convince myself that forgetting is a vocation that I am far too good at. I want a different calling—and I'm not talking about hanging up my stiletto heels. The story you're reading right now is not about how I exited the sex trade—it is the one I recount to remind myself that I survived and that the worth of my life can be paid back with my truth and my stories.

✦

Normally, when I speak about sex work, I conclude my narrative with a subtle or not-so-subtle call to action. I'll make recommendations about which sex workers' support organizations to donate money to. I might illuminate the difference between survival sex work and commercial sex work, decriminalization verses legalization, trafficking, child exploitation, and the many seemingly nuanced issues that are often lumped into the same controversial pile. I can tell you which members of parliament have moved sex workers' rights forward, and I can name the elected officials who seem content to let us die or go missing in the streets.

I do this because I grew up in a Silence = Death, direct action, *do something!* era. But I also believe that passively reading about or otherwise witnessing injustice injures us—it widens the disconnect. The part of us that is hurting does not heal in the dark; we must turn on the light to look at it. We must pay attention.

Right now, however, I will not beseech you to write a letter to your local politician or send a cheque to a local charity. Just for a moment, forget the donations or bylaw regulations, moral debates, social conservatism or what God thinks. Forget about hooker-with-a-heart-of-gold stereotypes. Survivor heroism—disregard that altogether. Save charity for another time. Charity is an "us" and "them" concept, after all, and even if you are in a financial position to give, what I'm asking for right now is the opposite of charity.

I'm asking you to entertain that wish I made earlier: to treat this like a two-way conversation. My dear reader, you've caught on by now that this is not really about sex work. Sex work is only one of many, many things that we learn we are not to talk about, one of many things we've been asked (but never agreed) to keep silent about.

This is about the labour of becoming whole and letting yourself see a wider panorama. It's about allowing yourself to listen to broader conversations—with your voice included—to visit the places that have been made silent or small or wounded.

Locate yourself within the bigger, puzzling, and sometimes hazardous world around you. You are invited to do this work. You are already doing this work. What combination of facts and lies represent you? What spectrum of identities do you hold dear while the larger world tells you that these identities don't even exist? What personal and public rituals do you perform to be seen? What truths must you create to fill the gaps? And what will you (you and I both) do with the knowledge we have (or haven't) been given?

For me, these questions are the same as poetry. They save me.

When this paragraph ends, this story is all yours.

INWARD

THERE ARE THE ROMANCES THAT STICK

to that song, that baby toe, that particular
hue of blue, that constant
twister of cherry blossoms in April on the corner
of Second and Commercial,
romances that stick to you long after they've ended—
and then there are the romances you barely remember at all.

They turn up in your memory like a key
found in the pocket of a coat you haven't worn for ages,
or a phone number scribbled on the last page of the self-help
book written by the Buddhist nun from Los Angeles
which you always fell asleep while reading, even on the bus,
and there is no name beside the number.

I don't remember the girl
whose father's front yard was strewn with Studebaker
and Bugatti skeletons, a battleground of chrome bones,
rusted limbs reaching for my ankles
as I snuck to her window at night. Her own
car was a Ford Galaxie 500, mint-green with a paler mint
interior, no radio, only distance
between us; those bucket seats so far apart.
The crickets' desperate hymn
along the back roads we drove, the sour smell
of sumac growing in the ditch, her cigarette
smoke floating above her like a halo that refused
to wholly commit itself to her head I remember,
but not her eyes, her clothes, the words she must have said,

or didn't.

I imagine this girl, now a woman,
has also forgotten the sterling silver eagle earrings
I wore every day that summer, the way August poured
freckles on my shoulders and nose, that I worked the snow
cone machine at a travelling fair and if they were going to Montana
I would go with them because I heard there was nothing
but fields of sunflowers there,

and I loved long drives
how you can close your eyes,

then open, and everything around you has changed.

THE ONE THING THAT COULD HAVE KEPT ME IN
FORT ERIE, ONTARIO

The year I left Fort Erie, Ontario—a border town flanking the Niagara River—its population was just over 20,000. There's still no movie theatre in my hometown. No chain coffee shops. Not one underground parking lot. The town library is a one-storey building (or two, if you count the sunken area where children's story-hour takes place).

Fort Erie is big in other ways. It sprawls sixty-four hay-seedy square miles. It can take half an hour to drive a car from one end of town to the other. Seniors, youth, and residents too broke to own a car—which is a fair number of folks—ride the FEPT: Fort Erie Public Transit or Fucking Excuse of a People Trolley as it is lovingly called by the townies. A single school bus, painted our official shade of royal blue, will pick you up just about anywhere from cow pasture to bingo hall between the hours of 7:30 a.m. and 7:30 p.m.

Fort Erieians can boast big backyards. Drag the lawnmower out of the garage in the morning and, by lunchtime, you've really earned that bologna sandwich and cold beer. My backyard spanned thirty-two acres of birch and cottonwood forest dotted with enough edible clover, choke cherries, and wild mushrooms to survive off for at least a few days. Living off the land was something of a family value. The Vietnam War, the Summer of Love, and Canada's then-Prime Minister Pierre Elliot Trudeau brought me to Fort Erie. Trudeau opened Canada's gates to the US's conscientious objectors to the Vietnam War, including my father, whose draft card was just about up. Ma and Pop met in 1969 and got married eight months later in Buffalo, NY. They drove across the Peace Bridge, signed some landed-immigrant documents at the border, and proceeded to an unspoiled stretch of land they and their hippie friends had optimistically purchased as a sanctuary for their turn-on, tune-in, and drop-out dreams.

What my parents didn't think through in their wonder years was how the fuck were they going to raise a teenaged daughter in the hellhole of Canada, a place where the top three activities for youth were fisticuffs in an empty lot, jumping off the train bridge into the rushing Niagara, or getting drunk on bootlegged gin, which the local barkeeps would sell to any kid with allowance money.

As in any riverside community, the Niagara propelled our stories, churned our small-town identities. As schoolchildren, we learned that the Iroquois—the First Peoples—called the river Ongniaahra: *that which cuts the land in two.* We were shown faded photos of horse ferries that really were powered by horses, each galloping alongside a wooden treadmill—town historians say those were tipsy boat rides. More harrowing still were the stories of the Underground Railway before the American Civil War. Thousands of enslaved Africans, with no more than the North Star to guide them, crossed the Niagara to whatever freedom Canada offered them. Our more progressive schoolteachers would take us on field trips to Freedom Park, where we would pray to God to end slavery forever, everywhere, *Jesus for justice.*

As high school students, we studied pollution; the Niagara River had been listed as an "area of concern" since the early 1900s. In the classroom, we read reports aloud about how the loss and deformation of fish and wildlife was bad. But when hanging out down by the river, we all swapped funny stories about the rainbow trout that was a little too rainbow-coloured, or the sheeps-head fish that bayed and croaked throughout the night. We dared each other to chug river water with our beer. We took turns dunking our heads under water and keeping our eyes open until they burned.

The Niagara River gave me my first orgasm, twelve miles from Devil's Hole, where the rapids can trick even a strong swimmer under the surface. I was skinny-dipping, drunk under a low-slung Indian summer moon, and found a warm current passing between an outcrop of limey boulders. There I wedged my fifteen-year-old body, my hands free to go wherever they wanted in the privacy of the black water's chop.

Across the river, the city lights of Buffalo winked at me: factories and freeways, nightclubs, art gallery steps, the illuminated rooftops of skyscrapers, and beyond Buffalo was Rochester, Syracuse, then New York, New York; bright lights, big city.

But I was stuck in Fort Erie. Endlessly tripping naked around the rocky riverbed toward the row of boys with whom I shared a bottle. Night after night, I latched onto their dark silhouettes and fucked and felt nothing more than an affinity with their neophyte machismo. I fucked in the blind hope that my ever-growing feelings of displacement could be fucked out of me. It did not work.

"You should get a job," my mother urged. She'd taken up the habit of looking into the distance when she spoke to me. She didn't want to see my dyed red hair and the second-hand lingerie I wore as a sundress. But she held my hand like she always had; her square meaty palms bigger than mine no matter how old I got. "Soon you'll graduate, then what?" she asked.

"Then I'll leave and never come back," I threatened.

"Well," Ma sighed. "You'd better save some money then."

I babysat and washed dishes at the Golden Palace Chinese Buffet, and a month after graduation (Class of '92), I worked the ticket booth at a carnival midway.

Every year for four days—Canada Day to the fourth of July—Mather Arch Park turns into an outdoor concert hall and carnival midway in celebration of the friendship between the US and Canada. Town officials make speeches about the War of 1812 and bagpipes play. What the Friendship Festival is all about is treating droves of Americans to a cheap Tom Cochrane concert and late-night beer tent.

Ma saw the help-wanted ad in the *Gazette* and drove me over to the park to stand in line with the rest of the teenagers and unemployed townies. A bleach-blonde in jean cut-offs handed me an application and a pen. "You sixteen?" she barked. "Gotta be at least sixteen." I dug into my studded purse for ID, but she moved down the line before I had the chance to show it to her.

"They act like they give two shits, but they don't," said the man with a farmer's tan ahead of me in line. "'Four-day idiots' they call us, because we do all the brainless jobs. Then they move on and get a new batch of townies to do their grunt work. Boss pays cash under the table; that's why we do this shit."

The boss's office was a dinged-up trailer with an eyeless clown painted on the side. The boss—a tall lanky man with a salt-and-pepper grey mullet—reviewed my application in less than three seconds. "Good with numbers?" He spoke in the same hurried bark as the blonde.

"Not bad," I shrugged.

"It takes two tickets to ride the Zipper and I want to ride it ten times. It's a dollar a ticket or fifteen bucks for a strip of twenty. What do you sell me?"

"A strip of twenty for fifteen bucks." I squirmed in the plastic chair, second-guessing myself.

"Right. And I got a twenty-dollar bill?"

"So you get five back or pick up an extra five tickets and ride some other rides or something?"

"Ticket booth," the boss mumbled.

"Ticket booth," the blonde, suddenly at the door, echoed as she led me by the elbow out of the trailer and across the half-constructed midway. Twisted tracks from the kiddie-coaster lay in pieces in the grass. Flattened inflatable fun houses were sad multi-coloured puddles waiting for an air pump.

"This is booth number three beside the carousel," said blondie, pointing at the motionless fibreglass horses. "Be right here at six o'clock tomorrow, got it?"

The next day, I discovered that blondie's name was Deb. Her bark had lengthened to a saccharine drawl—like a diner waitress in the movies—and marijuana perfumed her clothes. She unlocked the narrow back door of the orange shack that was booth number three. "This is it, honey," said Deb, motioning at the two bar stools, two metal lock boxes, and a poster of David Lee Roth in a snakeskin Spandex suit crammed inside the four-by-four-foot booth. She set me up with a dog-eared list of ticket prices, a calculator, and a cash float; new fives and tens spun through her vaudevillian fingers.

"You're good to go," she said slamming the cash box down on the tiny countertop. "Other girl gets here in half an hour. Show her what to do, okay, honey?"

Through the Plexiglas window, I watched Deb march across the grass, her backcombed hair bouncing with purpose. She weaved through the midway rides, neon lights flickered on in her wake, and by the time Deb finished her rounds, the entire park was a frenzied battle of classic rock vs. circus jingles, the alluring aromas of toasted caramel and corn dogs, and droves of hyper children hassling their parents for money. "Twenty tickets," they shouted at me through the circular cut-out in the Plexiglas, their brats bouncing around them like popcorn kernels.

Just as I noticed my foot starting to tap in time to the vexatious tune of the carousel, the other girl Deb had mentioned came pounding at the door. I flipped open the rusty latch to find Gina Costa standing outside, her hand poised mid-air, ready to pound some more. She was my enemy. We'd never scrapped it out after school; I had enough sense to avoid all five feet, eleven inches, and 170 pounds of her. But rumour had it that I was as good as toast ever since I'd made out with her gross ex-boyfriend at a bush bonfire party. We stood in silent deadlock for several long seconds. Mosquitoes buzzed past her through the open door and swirled around the flickering light bulb overhead. Bells frantically rung as someone won at the neighbouring duck-shoot game. Gina nervously bit her glittery lip-glossed lip, and I mustered the courage to say, "Whatcha going to do, throw down with me right here?" I turned my back to her before I had the chance to rethink my words. A crowd of eager kids was forming. As I slid the first boy his strip of tickets, Gina took her place on the adjacent stool.

The tiny booth was a tight fit for her, and she had to work pretty hard to keep her leg or shoulder from touching mine. She fussed with her spool of tickets as a few of the boys left my line and pressed themselves against her side of the window.

Gina was slow, or at least not as quick as I was with numbers. The solar calculator was nearly useless under the dirty low-watt bulb that hung above us. Maybe it was because I couldn't stand the line-up getting too long, or maybe it was my way of offering the olive branch, but I found myself gingerly dropping into her transactions, whispering, "Ten even. Break open the roll of loonies. American money is on par."

Apart from my muttered calculations, we did not speak until the very end of the night when Gina offered me a ride home. "Just don't laugh at my dad's heinous station wagon," she said.

"Um." The cashbox rattled in my hands. "My ma said she'd pick me up."

"'Kay," said Gina. "See ya tomorrow, then."

After she left, I compulsively recounted quarters and dimes. Beside me the stamp of Gina's thighs remained on the empty metal stool. I traced my index finger along the thin line of sweat where her inner thighs must have been, then fought the unsettling urge to stick my finger in my mouth. This is my first memory of a long-standing obsession with the lovely perspiration prints that sturdy girls who wear short skirts leave behind after sitting.

The next night, Gina and I were both itchy. Mosquito bites had claimed our bare legs and arms. "Quit scratching, you'll make them worse," I warned her. We spent our shift performing a pointless, jerky dance to keep Saturday's batch of mosquitoes from biting. Gina slapped one from my thigh, hard. "Look," she said, holding her hand up proudly, a smear of dead mosquito in her palm. "Gotcha!"

The night after, there were fireworks. With our foreheads against the Plexiglas, we struggled to see the red, white, and blue sparks just outside the view from the tiny booth window. I leaned back against the chipboard wall to see the bigger picture: a park full of people gazing up at the sky, couples—many couples—holding hands, girls with their heads tucked under their boyfriends' chins, fathers hoisting toddlers onto their shoulders with one arm, their others clapped around their young wives. I couldn't see what they were marvelling at; only the burnt-out fireworks floated by my vantage point as grey swaths of smoke. Jimmy—a high-school dropout who'd managed three dates out of me—was in the crowd with a tiny Goth girl hanging off him, and I bristled—not out of jealousy but from the thought that she was exactly what I must have looked like on his arm, a small, sloppy-drunk juvenile costumed in wannabe rebel's clothing.

"I hate it here," I told Gina.

"I don't mind if you go outside for a bit. Watch the fireworks," she offered.

"Not 'here', in this booth. I hate the whole fucking town."

She nodded in careless agreement and produced a twenty-sixer of cinnamon schnapps from her backpack. "Like my mom says, *buonanotte al secchio*."

"I don't speak *la lingua*."

"It means 'good night to the bucket', which means 'we're screwed.'"

"We're screwed," I toasted heartily, only to choke on my first sip.

"Don't get us caught, stupid," said Gina, snatching the bottle from my hands. Twisting her curvy weight, she squatted under the narrow countertop, out of site of the ticket window. I watched her throat quiver as she swallowed. A fat tear pushed itself out of the corner of her left eye. She pulled on my pant leg like a toddler and I squeezed down next to her on the booth's grimy floor. The bottle clinked against my teeth as Gina thrust it at me. "Ouch," I yelped and clapped my hand over my mouth.

"Baby," she hissed, but she placed a finger on my lip as if to check for blood. A second finger met my lip, then my chin was in her hand. Gina took a long swig of schnapps, tilted my head back, and cupped her lips over mine. Red-hot liquid ran from her mouth into mine. For a moment her sun-freckled arms were around me.

And a moment later, we were back to peddling tickets. Money moved through my hands mechanically. Flashing lights and whistles flogged our booth, making me claustrophobic and dizzy. Later still, I lay awake in my bed, raking my teeth over my cinnamon-tingly lips.

Running away with a carnival was neither a childhood dream nor nightmare of mine. I'd simply overheard Deb say that the carnival was moving next to Tonawanda, New York, then leaving Erie County altogether for Pennsylvania, Ohio, and who knew where next. I took up my plea with Deb.

"You gotta take me with you. I can't stay here one more day."

"Who's messing with ya? Is it your daddy?" Deb asked in a tone too casual for me to consider the appropriate reaction. I bowed my head and for a moment the trampled grass around my feet seemed to turn a devastating, electric green. Deb patted my shoulder. "I don't know my daddy, but my mom had plenty of boyfriends. A-holes, every one."

Deb marched me up to the boss's trailer before my last shift started. It was the fourth of July—the busiest night at the carnival, and I knew the boss wouldn't give us much time. "I just graduated with good grades. I can work pretty hard. And I'm already trained in the ticket booth," I made my case.

"Her cash is never short. I'd trust her with bank runs if I had to," Deb sided with me.

"Where she gonna sleep?" the boss asked Deb.

"I already told her she could bunk in my trailer. See how that goes," Deb told him.

"We clock some long days," said the boss, tapping a pen on his metal desk. "Get started before sun comes up some mornings. You gonna do that?"

"Sure thing," I said.

"A girl, a young girl like you, especially wearing those kinda get-ups"—the boss motioned to my bare legs, the row of safety pins that hemmed my short, short skirt—"can get into a lot of trouble. Trouble we ain't going to help you out with. Understand me?"

I nodded, coolly. I had already learned what the wrong side of the high school parking lot teaches. I already knew that no one helps girls with the kind of trouble we get into. But then I looked at Deb—the only woman carnie in the crew—with her ratted bangs that hung in her tired eyes. Her arms were always folded in front of her chest, her foot, always nervously tapping. Besides her sabre-toothed tiger tattoo, she was no different than the hard-bitten women who drank at the local bar in Fort Erie.

"Well, you've been warned. I suppose home is always just a bus ticket away," said the boss.

With that, Deb took a Polaroid picture of me holding my birth certificate and medical services CareCard, and I was officially a carnie, like her. "If you really want to do this, you be here by six a.m. tomorrow. Not a moment later."

After our shift, Gina and I ran for the Zipper, the ruthless king of midway rides. We'd spent nearly twenty-four hours at the carnival and hadn't gone on a single ride ourselves. "You girls are lucky. Last ride of the night goes to you," said the operator.

"Yeah, thanks. The Zipper is my favourite." Gina stuck her chest out as she spoke to him. It made me want to punch the carnie in his bearded face. He leered at her again as he checked the safety bar across our chests. He closed the heavy screen door and gave our cart a forceful push that sent us spinning upside down. The Zipper started with a beastly groan, and Gina and I grabbed each other without a thought of shyness. Her scream started off as rich and high as that uttered by the first slut to die in a slasher B-movie, but gave way to wheezing as we were tossed around in our metal cage. Her dry mouth met mine and we kissed clumsily until the Zipper groaned to a stop. The kiss was real this time. Even though we said nothing, we both knew it was real. I confessed to Gina that I'd be travelling on with the carnival. "Well, at least let me give you a ride home," she said finally.

I wanted to hold her hand as we crossed the midway toward the parking lot. Already the carnival was being torn down. The Fun House was being folded into wooden cargo boxes. Stray carousel horses lay on the dark lawn.

"My dad's car," Gina explained again, crinkling her nose up at the old station wagon with faux-wooden paneling. Some of the wood-grain veneer was peeling off around the edges. The hub caps were missing. Inside, the chocolate brown upholstery smelled faintly like feet.

Gina drove the back roads where few street lamps punctuated the night. There was the smell of sumac growing along the ditch, the sound of gravel pelting her back bumper, the occasional squeak of Gina's thighs against the vinyl seat.

"You're really going with the carnies?" she asked me.

"Ah, I don't know. They're creepy, right? But it's a way out of here." Like my parents had done twenty-some odd years before, I was ready to cross that border and never look back. *Do you want me to stay, Gina?* was the question caught on my tongue, and an older, braver me would have asked her. Instead I chattered away in teenage idiocy. I was still turning out some dumb response when Gina slammed on the breaks.

In the centre of the potholed road stood a barn owl, its white wings stretched out, challenging Gina's car, a small and mangled rodent in its claws. Screech owls, they're called in Southern Ontario; like the coyotes and night frogs, you can hear their strange sermons only after dark, but you rarely see one up close. But there was its heart-shaped face. Its moony eyes reflected the high beams. We held our breath. It flew off, and the night seemed all the blacker.

If there was uncertainty in Gina's eyes as I eased her T-shirt over her head, I could not see it. The freckles on her breasts, baby hairs below her belly button, birthmarks, scars, the colour of her nipples, I saw none of these. Just darkness. Small-town darkness. She said, "Oh," and, "This is crazy. This is crazy." I didn't need light for my hand to find its way into her cotton underwear. We didn't need words to know that only once in the bucket seat of her father's car was all we had.

Gina became a bank teller in downtown Fort Erie, had two kids and a husband before the age of twenty-two, and now owns a house with big backyard.

And me, I put in time with the carnival, then hitchhiked some, hopped a train once. The world soon proved that it was not so small. In turn, my young heart soon proved to hold more than wild angst and trouble. It took many women to teach me this lesson: how love can open you, lay you wider than dawn's horizon line. How the desire to find each other leads you forward. It is a road I doubt I'll ever quit travelling.

TO ALL THE BUTCHES I LOVED BETWEEN 1995 AND 2005: AN OPEN LETTER ABOUT SELLING SEX, SELLING OUT, AND SOLDIERING ON

You were a set of sturdy boys in well-worn Carhartt jeans and rock T-shirts. Rough scrubbed, each one of you, from your Brylcreemed hair to your polished black jump boots. You rode bellowing muscle bikes circa 1970s, drove cars with duct-tape interiors, or walked with practiced swaggers. You could hold your own at the pool table and in the kitchen—cooking your mamas' comfort-food recipes. You played "Ace of Spades" on electric guitar and hemmed your own pants. Your days were spent painting six-bedroom houses in Shaughnessy, tending to show-jumping horses, keeping university grounds, or otherwise soiling your fingers. You were evolved renditions of the very boy a small-town slut like me was expected to wind up with. But unlike that probable boyfriend, you were a feminist, you rejected the status quo with much greater consideration than it rejected you, and you didn't leave me a knocked-up single mother-to-be. I couldn't possibly have told you enough how truly remarkable you were.

To all the butches I loved between 1995 and 2005, there is a consequential and heartfelt queue of things I never said to you. Blame booze or youth, frequently practiced self-flagellation, homophobia, or any brew of stinking societal influences for me holding my tongue. What matters now is that I put some honest words to our past and—if the graces allow—that you will hear me.

If the details are a blur (and I don't blame you if they are), let me remind you that I was your girl, your mommy, your headache, or your heart song (depending on my mood). On a good day I wrote poetry, walked rescue dogs, or led survivors' support groups at the women's centre. I'd all but quit rush drugs, but on a bad day I drank like a fancy fighting betta fish in a small bowl. I spent my nights gliding around softly lit massage parlours in a pair of glitter-pink stilettos. Personal economics informed my femme identity. My transition took place in prudent increments: I grew my neon-orange dyke hair into a mane of bleach blonde; I shaved my armpits and pussy; I dieted down to 100 pounds, and, in effect, I learned to indulge the tastes of men with money to spend. When the business was good, I made more in an hour than you did all week.

This is where my overdue disclosures begin. Whenever I picked up the dinner tab or put gas in your tank, we'd both swallow a quiet shame. I might have mumbled something aloof like, "Easy come, easy go," handling the neatly folded bills with the same cool discretion as my male customers did when they paid me.

For a good long time, I positioned this shame entirely in a have-and-have-not credo. I believed that all my shame came from the very same stomping grounds as my pride: from my humble class background.

I've since realized that this summation is too easy.

You and I and just about everyone we knew were salt-of-the-earth folk. Salt of the earth meets pervert, that is, on account of us being the kind of kinky, tough-love queers that set us apart from our back-home birth families. Ours was an elbow-grease, adult-children-of-alcoholics, there-ain't-no-such-thing-as-a-free-lunch butch-femme. That's right, let's say it again. Ours was a damaged-goods, bitter-pill, better-luck-next-time butch-femme. We were cut from the same threadbare cloth, and we wore it well. Our world was filled with modest, yet revered, codes and traditions. When guests came over, they were offered mismatched kitchen chairs to sit on. If there was whiskey in the cupboard, it was either

Jim or Jack. Clothing was swapped. Tools were shared. There were logging-road camping trips and back-alley bonfires. We danced like crazy in creaky-floored rental rec centres and declining dance halls; we'd make the air hot and muggy, the old wood floors stickier than fly paper. And in the dark safe corners of the night, we fucked with our fists, teeth, and hearts like we were indestructible. This was our behind-the-eight-ball butch-femme. I was never ashamed of it.

The shame I felt came from sex work. There it is, as barefaced as it can be. Don't get me wrong, I still wear my feminist-slut badge. This isn't some dubious argument between the merits of waiting tables for minimum wage versus the formidable money-making of prostitution. Morals are not being re-examined. I'm not moving from "camp empowerment" to "camp victim" (such dichotomies are far too short-sighted to sum up sex workers). What I'm coming out about is that sex work changed my relationship with being a working-class femme and, in turn, my relationship with you, my butch lovers.

Sometimes you tried to talk about it. I want to thank you for being brave enough to speak up, even though you didn't always say the right thing. I remember waking up one morning to your big green eyes. You had been watching me sleep since sunrise, adoringly at first, the way smitten lovers do, then your thoughts took a turn and you began to wonder, "How the heck is this my girlfriend?" Fake tan, synthetic hairweave, fake, long airbrushed fingernails; you said that lying beside me felt "surreal." I suppose I looked like a poster child for the beauty myth we had been warned about in our early 1990s feminist education. I looked like the kind of femme who is dubbed "high maintenance" or "princess"—indeed these labels were used to describe me—though the reality was that sex work had only made me tougher and more fiercely independent. Still, there wasn't anything punk rock or edgy, humble, or even queer about my exterior femme persona. I pretty much looked like I belonged in a chat-line or diet-pill commercial. The familiar fit of you and me (your butch and my femme) had been disrupted. Had I sold out our butch-femme codes? Had I snuck the bourgeoisie "other" into our bed?

"I make more money when I look like this." How frequently I used this disclaimer. It was fractured thinking I employed as a sex worker: there was the persona and then there was the real me. But, as I've already mentioned, easy dichotomies fall short. As with my appearance, sex work began to reshape my life. Prostitution money paid for my liberal arts degree, followed by an MFA in creative writing. If I was going to be the college-student-by-day, working-girl-by-night cliché, I was determined to average at least a 4.0—even if it meant turning a date with a dental student during lunch break so I could pay for my biology tutor that same afternoon. I was raised with the principle of sacrifice; if I was going to obtain the things that my class background hadn't afforded me, I figured I was bound to suffer at least a little.

While I'd grown somewhat accustomed to grappling with the personal sacrifices that came with sex work, witnessing your inner conflict was an entirely different challenge. Although we both agreed in theory that my job ought to be treated like any other line of work, if your boss called to offer you an extra shift, the biggest conundrum was whether or not the overtime would cut into our upcoming scheduled dates. "Baby, you don't mind, do you?" was all you needed to say, conversation closed. In contrast, entire nights seemed to be ruined when my madam called to ask me to take a last-minute client. As I'd whisper into my cell phone, I witnessed your face stiffen. Eventually, the sound of my ringtone alone was a cause for pause.

I never had to lie to my friends about what you did for a living. "She's a carpenter" or a "welder-in-training," I boasted. These were strong, rugged, and proudly butch professions. Telling people that your girlfriend was a sex worker was a crapshoot, at best. Of course, there were our close mutual friends who I was out to. Others were told a half-truth: that I was a stripper rather than a full-fledged, blowjob-performing prostitute. This explanation spared you from uttering an outright lie and also from making your buddies uncomfortable or concerned. What kind of man dates a prostitute? He is considered either a tyrant, a pimp, or a broken man who can't take care of his woman. Our radical queer values didn't protect us from these stigmas. "I wish I could protect you" was another brave thing that you frequently said to me. I took what comfort I could in this sentiment and let you wrap your arms around me a little tighter. This tender statement, however, affirmed how truly uncomfortable you were with sex work and, worse still, how uncomfortable you were that my work made you feel powerless. Butches aren't "supposed" to feel powerless. I was inadvertently de-butching you. And, as a femme who believes (and celebrates) that her role as a femme is to make her butch feel like one hell of a butch, I was de-femme-ing myself, too.

Sex work changed the way I fucked. Confessions don't come any harder than this one.

I remember the first time I refused to kneel for you. We were making out at one of our fuck spots, between a row of high-school portables a few blocks from your house. You took out your cock, ran your thumb along my bottom lip, and yanked my hair as you did when you wanted me on the ground. It was Friday night. The next day was my regular Saturday shift, when all the big-tipping clients visited the massage parlour, and I couldn't risk having my knees scraped like a "cheap whore." It might have messed with my money. Moreover, I refused to reveal the real me at work. My work persona didn't have scraped knees (or welts or hickies, etc.).

The simplest, sexiest diversion would have been to spit on your cock and lift my skirt. Instead, I stood there frozen in that inciting moment when I realized that keeping my real life and work neatly separated was impossible; it was failing at every opportunity. Sex work was not simply coating the surface of my body like a topcoat of glitter nail polish. It had sunk in.

We could playfully liken my appearance to a drag queen's. My money financed more than a few good times together. But we met an impasse when the impact of sex work entered our bedroom. Setting boundaries around scraped knees was only a preview to long and recurring phases where I couldn't be touched at all. Contrary to your fantasies and my own, I wasn't an inexhaustible source of amorous coos and sighs. My pussy was not an eternal femme spring, always wet and ready. These coquettish images may sound overblown, but they were critical to our relationship. They were critical to who I was as a femme. I hadn't chosen the saccharine country classic "Touch Your Woman" by Dolly Parton (my working-class femme role model) as a mantra for nothing! Who was I, as a femme, if I couldn't offer my body to you, my butch lovers, as a touchstone, a safe haven of hotness, a soft-skinned, sweet-mouthed reminder that who we were was right and good?

A bigger question: what the heck did sex between us look like if I wasn't going to spread my legs anymore? Most of you had your own set of complex raw spots—as our generation of butches with hard-knock pasts often do. I'd spent my younger femme years devotedly learning about and responding to the nuanced body language and boundaries of butches. Suddenly, it was all I could do to keep up with my own changing limits and body issues.

For awhile I tried on "stone femme" as an identity. In many ways, this label protected me and made me feel powerful. It also became a regular topic for dissection in our small community. "A stone femme, meaning a femme who loves stone butches?" I was asked repeatedly.

"No, I mean I myself am stone," I'd say. "I don't let lovers touch me."

"Hmm." I got a lot of doubtful "hmms" in response, as if I was speaking in riddles.

Ultimately, changes to the way I fucked meant we both had to reinvent the codes and traditions of the butch-femme bedroom as we knew them, which under different circumstances might have been a fun task, but the possibilities weren't as discernible as the losses. The question "Could we …?" was not asked as often as "Why can't we …?"

Let's just skip the berating part, where I say, "I admit I wasn't always an easy woman to stand beside." Let's move right to the part where I simply thank you for doing so. If you've hung on and heard me this far, then please let me finish this letter by explaining exactly what it is I am thanking you for.

You were adaptable. You tried really darn hard to be adaptable. Most of the time this only made you about as flexible as a flagpole, but I noticed you bend and knew that you did it for me. I remember the time you let me strap it on and be the first femme to fuck you. It ranks quite high up in my list of favourite all-time memories. Later, you gloated to your butch buddies, "She's more 'butch' than me between the sheets." To my surprise, comradely arm-punching and shared stupid grins followed this admission. It made me wonder if you needed that fuck (and those that followed) as desperately as I did. Maybe you needed a damaged-goods, stone femme like me to ask you to become something besides the ever-infallible butch top you were accustomed to being.

Likewise, maybe you needed to cry with me during those rare times when you resisted the urge to take up the emotional reins and say, "Baby, don't cry" or, "It will be okay." This was a delicate and extraordinary space, when we both unabashedly cried together. For me, this was the emotional antithesis of the wordless reactive shame I often felt but lacked the guts or words to talk about. Thank you for sharing this space with me.

There were many moments when I doubted myself during those years—hazardous moments, like brushes with bad clients, when yours were the strong arms in which I sought respite. There were also many instances when I lacked the confidence to walk with dignity into a university classroom or a square job interview, moments when I was tempted to blow my ho money by going on benders because climbing the class ladder was terrifying. Thank you for loving me the way you knew best. Your big calloused hands held me strong to this life. You still took me dancing until our clothes were soaked through with sweat. You popped Heart's *Greatest Hits* in your car stereo, and we drove the back roads singing "Crazy on You" in comically awful dis-harmony. You called me "old lady" and "beautiful" and "my girl." You taught me that butch-femme wasn't about dress codes, the gendered skills we'd acquired, or jobs we held, or even about who bent over in the bedroom. At the crux of it all, our butch-femme traditions were about creating a place that was distinctly ours. Again and again you brought me to this home, this shelter from external pressures, this asylum from troubled pasts and uncertain futures. Thank you for assuring me that I always had a remarkable, shameless place.

...AND WE DID

I have stood naked on the art gallery's steps.

We were one hundred strong, lesbians,
we seized the food court at the Pacific Centre mall to disrupt
the heteronorm with an anti-homophobia kiss-in.

I have kissed pavement while an officer handcuffed me
another searched my bra and underpants for an alleged weapon.
(No one read me my rights. No weapons were found.)

Our rubber-soled boots tracked red footprints down
the highway onramp. Vaseline will help
break down spray paint stains on skin—*share this information.*
Our mark the next morning: shame / stop / smash / the state
vote no / yes / now / rƎVO⅃ution.

We ate pepper spray.
We saw riot tanks rush London on Financial Fools Day.
I have torn a sleeve from my blouse and used it to bind
an open wound.
Once, I sat in a cake at a charity ball where the mayor
was in attendance.

Before the Internet we found each other in the streets like swallows
who find their way home each summer. How did we know?

We linked arms. A human chain, we chanted *the people*
united will never be defeated.
We were young. So certain we would change the world ...

We were young. So certain we would change the world…
The people united will never be defeated.
We chanted. A human chain, we linked arms.

How did we know to find each other like swallows
in the summer?
Before the internet we made our home in the streets.

I once sat in a cake at a charity ball where the mayor
was in attendance.
I once tore a sleeve from my blouse and used it to dress
an open wound.
We saw riot tanks rush London on Financial Fools Day.
We ate pepper spray.

shame / stop / smash / the state / vote no /
yes / now / rƎVO⅃ution: our mark.
In the morning, share this information.
Vaseline breaks down the spray paint stains
on skin and rubber-soled boots.
We tracked red footprints down the highway onramp.

(No one read us our rights. No weapons were found.)
We have kissed pavement while officers handcuffed us,
others searched our bras and underpants for the alleged weapons.

We seized the food court at the Pacific Centre mall to disrupt
the heteronorm with an anti-homophobia kiss-in.
We were one hundred strong, lesbians!

I have stood naked on the art gallery's steps.

INWARD

SELF-ADDRESSED POSTCARDS

1. *La Bastille*

There is nothing wrong with the sound of high heels chiming up the steps of the Voltaire station. You are indebted to this city for its fashion. Like other tourists, you pose beneath the Métro sign in your summer dress, muse over the romantic snippets of history you've managed to retain. Louie XIV. The Marquis de Sade. The French Revolution. Imprisoned poets. "If I were not king, I should lose my temper." And "It is always by way of pain one arrives at pleasure." And what was it that Voltaire said about pardoning error and loving truth? Paris tilts your head back as if for a kiss, dizzies you with its relentless baroque skyline. Submit to being lost.

Then, when you turn down Rue des Taillandiers, you know just where you are. Women wait in a snaking line for their Saturday night to start. Smoke floats above their fedora-clad heads, their lackadaisical haircuts. Women hug the thumping façade of Les Disquaires, corralled into a tight twelve feet of pavement behind a predictably dingy velvet rope. A snug space you dovetail yourself into as a matter of practice, familiar with how balmy summer heat is shared between bodies. The butch at the door epitomizes a butch at a door. She could be the gatekeeper to any dyke bar anywhere, with her cigarette pack deftly rolled into her T-shirt sleeve, nautical stars tattooed over each elbow. She chuffs at your Canadian passport.

Inside, women are lumped shoulder to shoulder. Feet upon feet. French chatter convenes into a single blaring noise. Whiskey and ginger is only five Euros if you ever get the bartender's attention. Better order two, double fist. One glass grows warm in your hand while you empty the other a fast as you can. You snatch up one of the few bar stools, sit and stare at the looping projection on the far wall. The phrase "What's *Gouine* On?" flashes enough times that even you (an outsider anglophone) catch the joke. There's too much going on. Strobe lights, overdone. Electro-pop overkill. And too many *gouines* (translation: "lesbians") for you to gouge one out the crowd. You've never been good at cruising clubs. The thing of it is, everyone says French girls are easy. What does it mean if you can't pick up in Paris? Do you get to call yourself a slut anymore? You force yourself from your perch, slightly less sure of your feet after two cocktails, and make for the dance floor.

The DJ is not going to play Katy Perry so you must work with the Eurodance kick. Synthetic bass drum makes the women bounce. No room to bust out your booty, only the hyper-tight tempo, up and down, down and up. Someone runs a cold beer bottle along your arm. Not the kind of come-on you wish to entertain, but it makes you aware of the possibilities. Another dances behind you for a moment, her hand lands on your hip then takes off again. You've got your eye on the one in the polka-dot blouse. She is just the type of femme you're always trying to ask out. She is just the type of femme that always thinks your invitation is only a "friend date." She notices you looking and undoes a button as she approaches. *All that cleavage just for me*, you swoon. You lock pinkie fingers like little girls. Your first kiss is not so sweet. Tongue and teeth at once. Raw kiss. You can't understand a word she is saying.

Through crudely pieced-together communications, she agrees to being taken outside and fucked in the street. Le Bastille has turned lamplight blue and almost lonely. The only sound comes from other couples tucked into doorways and dark corners. "All you have to do is hold your skirt up and look pretty," you tell her. You want her to have something to do with her hands besides touch you.

Triggers follow you, even to Paris, and this impending scene with this heartthrob femme is too hot to risk spoiling by setting off your booby-trapped body. She lifts her skirt like a can-can dancer. Her stockings catch on the stucco wall you push her against. If she's like you, she knows stockings are a common sacrifice. You brace your left arm behind the small of her back to cushion her. Each time she grinds, stucco grates your forearm. Her lace underwear is too perfect around her knees for you to worry over a few scratches. She says, "You can fuck me, okay," which makes you stall so she'll say it again. For a second you press your bare knuckles between her legs to feel if she's wet before fishing a glove from your purse. Suddenly you can smell her. Not just her nearly dripping cunt, all of her. Smoke on her clothes. White wine on her breath. You nuzzle into her hair—her fruity shampoo gives you a head rush. Her teeth clamp down on your neck as you slide another finger inside her. "More, please. More fingers." Already she is taking four. "Fist?" you ask. She presses her smeared-lipstick lips together. You're unsure if she is thinking it over or if she doesn't understand. "Fist?" you ask again. You tease her clit with your thumb, nothing further. She says, "I never tried fist." You hold so still you can feel the pulse in your jaw palpitating. The broken-language negotiation pauses. She wriggles her body down, grabs your wrist and steers your hand inside her. "Okay," she says. Her knees tremble. You watch her underwear fall around her ankles in cinematic slow motion.

"Okay," she echoes, more urgently. "*Fort!*"—one of a few French words you recognize. You punch into her. Feel her open up so that you can punch harder. She releases your wrist and thrusts her hand inside your shirt, wrestles with your bra to find your breasts. Your "no" catches in your throat. See how much she is offering, how truly beautiful her willingness is. She makes pleasure seem so effortless, so unburdened. What if you let down your guard? The moment you decide to surrender some of your stone-femme boundaries, her cunt tightens. She presses her palm against your chest as she comes. You imagine her *joie de vivre* passing from her fingers into your skin, past your breastbone and ribs, deeper. She says, "Thank you." You answer, *"Je devrais vous remercier."* Strangers, neither of you knowing quite what you've given each other.

2. Everyone Hearts a Virginia Girl

Splat! is the sound of your ejaculate hitting a cold bathroom floor in a sorority house in eastern Virginia. Like a comic-book hero punching the villain in the face. Just like that. Splat! But you can't begin a story at the climax. Go back to the part where Bill O'Reilly falsely accuses you of soliciting students across the US and offering sexual services for pay on campuses. Back to the part where Bill O'Reilly momentarily turns his attention away from slandering pro-choice supporters and Muslim communities and focuses his Fox News Channel hatred on you. Not only you, but the entire passenger van of artists you travel with: writers, musicians, burlesque and modern dancers, performance artists, visionaries. You are part of a neo-cabaret troupe called the Sex Workers' Art Show, and right-wing nuts are tailing you as you drive Highway 95.

Back up even further to explain the show's credo: "To dispel the myth that people who work in the sex industry are anything short of artists, innovators, and geniuses." Kids on campuses are listening. From UCLA to Harvard, they pool their student activity money, their women's studies and health centre money, their bake-sale fundraiser money to bring the show to their schools. After each standing-room-only performance, there is always the young woman waiting for you at the merch table. She starts to cry as she shakes your hand. You understand that she is like you—that campuses are populated with many women who, just like you, pay for a higher education through their skin and secrets. This is why you write, why you agreed to tour thirty-one cities in thirty-five days in a packed passenger van, so that you can be here to tell this young woman that she is not alone.

Now white-washed Colonial homes and imposing black willows appear to be scrutinizing you as you pull up to the university theatre. There are police cars in the parking lot. Religious protesters pray on the lawn. A trinity of malicious and misleading media—*The O'Reilly Factor*, *The 700 Club*, and *Christianity.com*—has armed the locals with fervid figurative pitchforks. You stare at the sidewalk as you rush inside, successfully ignoring the un-welcoming committee flanking the theatre entrance, then hide in the greenroom all night, anxiously reading and re-reading your set. Backstage your tour mates hug one another in solidarity. When onstage, you are grateful that the spotlight washes the audience away. After the final bow, when the houselights go dark, a smiling young woman approaches you. She says, "My sisters and I are having a party tonight. Would you and the other performers like to come?"

For a moment you and your tour mates stand on the sorority house stoop and wonder if you're about to fall victims to some cruel prank. Is this a trap? Are you about to be backslapped by good old conservative Christian hospitality? Instead, applause greets you as you come through the door. Fifty students or more with their glasses raised in the air. The first thing you notice is that the carpet smells like beer. There is a cigarette-burned, upside-down American flag tacked to the wall. Your Hollywood movie delusions sink into the mismatched sofas—you thought all sorority houses were like the pink-perfect film set of *Legally Blonde*. Why would anyone spend thousands of dollars to live in a house so drafty that you have to keep your coat on inside? The woman with the big smile and rugby-player shoulders offers you a drink you cannot identify. "We're so glad you came," she says. "They tried to force us to cancel the show. The fight's gone on for weeks." *The fight could go on for a lifetime*, you think. When you kiss her, the other students holler like it's spring break.

The light bulb is burned out in the bathroom where she leads you. In the darkness she becomes only a soft voice asking for permission to take your pants down. You grab onto what feels like a towel bar, rest your forehead on the tiled wall, and tell her, "Yes." Rather than concentrating on her hand on your ass, your mind begins an involuntary loop of enemy sound bites, the blog comments and radio segments you tried so hard to ignore:

"Is what an escort thinks about now considered meaningful education? Is watching hookers the sort of learning activity taxpayers had in mind? If Thomas Jefferson knew the school he attended was using public funds for smut, he'd just burn the place to the ground. This institution is no different from other universities in this nation—a breeding ground for socialists and the terminally brain-washed. Educrats can be very open-minded when it comes to degeneracy. Now that the anti-war movement has won the endorsement of the sex industry, they will be unstoppable. Maybe these so-called sex workers can teach the Democratic Party to become whores for Al-Qaeda?"

Your pussy wants nothing to do with America's founding fathers or present-day warmongers. Eject all this bullshit from your body. Empty the defamations from your mind. Drop back into the scene where your hair is tangled up in a kindred fist. She jerks your head back so she can kiss your cheek. What a basic and intimate act—a kiss on the cheek. Her lips are exceptionally warm in the dark damp room. It's then you feel the goose bumps tingling up the back of your thighs. You realize she's made a wet mess between your legs. You hear yourself scream. Sucker-punch orgasm—you didn't see it coming. Then her arms around you, like she's holding you upright. She laughs, "I think we made a lot of noise," as the party carries on just outside the bathroom door.

3. Sweet Home
—for my wife

Four summers together and you are still surprised by her hand on the nape of your neck.

You met during an uncommonly beautiful May. Vancouver's persistent cloud cover was driven off by warm El Niño winds, leaving the view postcard perfect. Snow-capped mountains, sun-beaded sea, and so many azaleas and hawthorn flowers that the city seemed to be blushing. Your first date found you swimming in your underwear off a glacial scour, the sloping shoreline of Horseshoe Bay. "It's not normally like this. It's normally too cold," you told her as you slipped into the black water. You didn't know she was afraid of the ocean. She didn't know that you are afraid of Christmas; that you never turn your back to the only exit in a room; how sometimes you don't leave your house for days; about your fear of being touched on the back of your neck or, periodically, being touched at all; that you navigate this world like trouble is around every corner; that you often worry that being tough is the closest you'll get to being happy.

Why is it you've written so much about desire and very little about love? Don't blame it on abstraction. You've mustered up a million examples of actualizing other emotions, and by now you are well aware that poetry can make even the highest concepts concrete. No, you don't write about love for the very same reason you refuse to learn to roller skate. You dislike the idea of introducing anything that requires hurting yourself repeatedly before you get good at it. You are reluctant to fall on your ass. But hasn't she left a fine filigree of welts on your ass? Did you not ask to wear her teeth marks like ornaments around your neck? Have you not limped through your days appreciatively sore from her fucking you? This newfound willingness to give yourself you chalked up to love at first sight. What is closer to the bone is that right away you sensed her love was forceful enough to turn you inside out. And you wanted to have the contents of your heart shaken out. You wanted to be emptied, so that, gradually, you could replace old, persistent fears with her love.

In the room you've made together, there is an east-facing window. Through this window you've watched the moon disappear and return a hundred times before you understood the message. There is artistry to self-perpetuation—the moon's had a lot of practice. You, however, are a still tenderfoot when it comes to beginning again. Now you stand in this world as someone who is completely loved. From this point of view, who knows what poetry is yet to come?

PUBLICATION CREDITS

The following pieces were previously published:
"How to Bury Our Dead" in *Second Person Queer* (Arsenal Pulp Press, 2009); "To All the Butches I Loved Between 1995 and 2005: An Open Letter About Selling Sex, Selling Out, and Soldiering On" in *Persistence: All Ways Butch and Femme* (Arsenal Pulp Press, 2011);"Oral Tradition" in *Event*, 37.2, 2008; "Sex Worker's Feet" in *Dandelion*, 27.1, 2001; "Ghetto Feminism" in *Room*, 30.2, 2007; "Melhos Place" in *subTerrain*, 52, 2010; "How I Got My Tattoo" in *Poetry Is Dead*, 3, 2012.

AMBER DAWN is a writer, filmmaker, and performance artist. Author of the Lambda Literary Award-winning novel *Sub Rosa*, she has an MFA in Creative Writing (UBC); her award-winning short film *Girl on Girl* was screened in eight countries and added to the gender studies curriculum at Concordia. Until August 2012, she was director of programming for the Vancouver Queer Film Festival. Amber Dawn was the 2012 winner of the Writers' Trust of Canada Dayne Ogilvie Prize for LGBT writers.